›› Praise for *Your Next Big Thing* ‹‹

"Very many people from all walks of life feel anxious, frustrated, and 'stuck' in their lives and can't see a way forward. As a clinical psychologist, Ben Michaelis knows this all too well. Often enough the prescription is clear. We create our lives and we can re-create them too. The best way ahead is to look within ourselves and rekindle our natural appetites for imagination, play, and a driving sense of purpose. Based on his extensive experience as a practicing therapist, *Your Next Big Thing* is a highly practical and delightfully readable guide to how to make the most of your life by making the best of yourself."

—**Sir Ken Robinson**, Educator and *New York Times* Bestselling Author of
The Element: How Finding Your Passion Changes Everything (Viking)

"Dr. Michaelis has created a manual for changing your life that is effective, practical, and holistic. He invites us to befriend our demons so as to liberate our true essence and live a life of joy and meaning. His writing is down-to-earth and humorous. You can trust him as your guide if you are feeling stuck or uninspired and even if you are on purpose and simply want a friendly voice to keep you on track."

—**Hala Khouri**, MA, Somatic Counselor, Yoga Teacher,
and Co-founder of Off the Mat, Into the World®

"Ben Michaelis has written a wonderfully practical and inspiring guide to living a life of purpose and creativity. Whether one is stuck or seeking to enhance an already satisfying life, Ben's thought-provoking and clarifying exercises, concrete strategies, and real-life examples help the reader reflect, prioritize, and take action."

—**Martha E. Edwards**, PhD, Director of the Ackerman Institute for
the Family's Center for the Developing Child and Family

"*Your Next Big Thing* is a groundbreaking and essential book. With his approachable and empathic style, Dr. Michaelis gives you the tools and confidence you need to awaken your passions and forge a new path to your future."

—**Jordan Matter**, Photographer and Author of
Dancers Among Us (Workman Publishing)

"Ben's book is a gift to everyone who is stuck . . . . For the price of two frappuccinos, this book will change your life. Seems like a good investment to me."

—**Nancy Lublin**, CEO of Do Something and Author of
Zilch: The Power of Zero in Business

"Dr. Ben Michaelis truly embodies his philosophy of play throughout both his personal and his professional life. He shows us each how play and self-expression can bring meaning and fulfillment to our lives on many levels."

—**Cricket Azima**, Big Cheese and Founder of The Creative Kitchen and Kids Food Festival

"*Your Next Big Thing: 10 Small Steps to Get Moving and Get Happy* is an amazing book that brings many aspects of self-development together in the most simple and yet powerful way. Dr. Michaelis has an amazing way of translating complex psychological concepts into simple steps easy to follow and does so in a very engaging and personal conversational style that makes the reader feel at ease and connected."

—**Dinelia Rosa, PhD**, Director of the Dean-Hope Center of Educational & Psychological Services, and Adjunct Associate Professor at the Clinical Psychology Program at Teachers College, Columbia University

"After many years of practicing psychotherapy, Dr. Michaelis brings his deep knowledge of human suffering, his accumulated clinical wisdom, and his finely tuned astuteness to bear on helping people who are stuck and frustrated in various aspects of their lives. Using a series of succinct quizzes, he enables the reader to identify problematic areas in living and offers extremely thoughtful guidance about how to emerge from and overcome various emotional traps. Although there have been numerous self-help books over the years, this one stands out as truly exceptional. It is clearly written, jargon-free, and should have a powerful transformative effect for those who immerse themselves in it and are receptive to the guidance it offers. The '10 Small Steps' Dr. Michaelis offers promise to put you on the path to greater happiness and personal fulfillment."

—**David L. Wolitzky, PhD**, Former Director of the Clinical Psychology PhD Program, New York University, Supervisor of the New York University Postdoctoral Program in Psychotherapy and Psychoanalysis

"*Your Next Big Thing* is a great step-by-step, interactive guide for getting 'unstuck' and moving forward in life."

—**Guy Winch, PhD**, Author of *The Squeaky Wheel*

YOUR NEXT BIG THING

Reimagine Yourself »» Discover Your Purpose »»
Take Action »» **LIVE IN THE NOW**

10
MALL STEPS TO **GET MOVING** AND **GET HAPPY**

Ben Michaelis, PhD

Aadamsmedia
Avon, Massachusetts

Published by
Adams Media, a division of F+W Media, Inc.
57 Littlefield Street, Avon, MA 02322. U.S.A.
www.adamsmedia.com

ISBN 10: 1-4405-4076-4
ISBN 13: 978-1-4405-4076-9
eISBN 10: 1-4405-4191-4
eISBN 13: 978-1-4405-4191-9

Printed in the United States of America.

10   9   8   7   6   5   4   3   2   1

Library of Congress Cataloging-in-Publication Data

Michaelis, Ben.
Your next big thing / Ben Michaelis.
p. cm.
Includes index.
ISBN 978-1-4405-4076-9 (hardcover) – ISBN 1-4405-4076-4 (hardcover) – ISBN
978-1-4405-4191-9 (ebook) – ISBN 1-4405-4191-4 (ebook)
1. Self-actualization (Psychology) 2. Success–Psychological aspects. 3. Success
in business. I. Title.
BF637.S4M488 2012
158–dc23
2012027860

This publication is designed to provide accurate and authoritative information with regard to the subject matter covered. It is sold with the understanding that the publisher is not engaged in rendering legal, accounting, or other professional advice. If legal advice or other expert assistance is required, the services of a competent professional person should be sought.

—From a *Declaration of Principles* jointly adopted by a Committee of the American Bar Association and a Committee of Publishers and Associations

Many of the designations used by manufacturers and sellers to distinguish their product are claimed as trademarks. Where those designations appear in this book and Adams Media was aware of a trademark claim, the designations have been printed with initial capital letters.

This book is available at quantity discounts for bulk purchases.
For information, please call 1-800-289-0963.

DEDICATION

For Carrie
First. Last. Only. Always.

ACKNOWLEDGMENTS

Many people helped make this book a reality, either through inspiring me, pushing the manuscript forward, or supporting my efforts with advice, guidance, or good vibes. I will use the next few paragraphs to acknowledge these contributions, but my words will be poor substitutes for my genuine gratitude.

Thank you to the early adopters and those who have inspired me near and far: Julie Miesionczek, Marc Haeringer, Ed Claflin, Trina Kaye, Tara Sweeney, Greg Mortimer, Evan Bachner, Ed Rivera, DLL, Rachel Garrett, Justin Garrett, Dave Ayala, Dave Adox, Karen Marder, Andrew Morrel, PhD, Ankur Saraiya, MD, Jason Diaz, Stephanie B. Levey, PhD, and Hannah Zimpritch.

Thank you to my family: Mom, Dad, Eden, Steve, Cheri, and of course, Juliet and Charlie.

A special thank you to Rachel Bressler, who has been promoting this project with fierce fury.

Thank you to everyone at Adams Media for working on this book, but especially Victoria Sandbrook for taking a risk on a first-time author, and Peter Archer, who helped immeasurably with the development of the final manuscript.

Finally, thank you to all of the people whom I have ever had the honor of working with—you continually guide, teach, and inspire me. You have shown me that there truly is a hero inside all of us and that if we let him lead us, he can take us to amazing places.

CONTENTS

Introduction 9

CHAPTER 1:   Running in Place 11

PART I: Knowing Your Path 29
CHAPTER 2:   Know Yourself 30
CHAPTER 3:   Imagine Yourself 47
CHAPTER 4:   Discover Your Purpose 68

PART II: Facing Your Demons 83
CHAPTER 5:   Face Your Inner Critic 84
CHAPTER 6:   Take Action 106
CHAPTER 7:   Embrace Your Process 132
CHAPTER 8:   Defeat the Three-Headed
             Monster 145

PART III: Walking Your Path 169
CHAPTER 9:   Reclaim Your Inner Hero 170
CHAPTER 10: Live in the Now 188
CHAPTER 11: Share Yourself 207

CHAPTER 12: Moving with Purpose 220

Index 236
About the Author 240

Hello. Welcome to *Your Next Big Thing.*

Whether you are checking out this book online, flipping through it in a bookstore or library, or just found it holding up some shelves in your friend's kitchen, you were drawn to it because you want to know something—something, I daresay, about your next big thing. That's convenient, because that's exactly what this book is about: you and your future.

These are trying times, and whether you have spent years precisely calculating your next move or you hadn't considered the future until the moment you came across this book, thinking about your horizon can be confusing and frightening. The only thing that is certain about the future is that it is *un*certain. However, if you know yourself, have an image of what you want your life to look like, and are armed with strategies for how to make it happen, you can face your next big thing with greater self-awareness, confidence, and faith.

The ideas, quizzes, and strategies in the pages ahead are all designed to help you think about who you are, where you want to be, and how to get you there. This book is about bringing all of you—not part, not some, but *all* of you—into the present so that you can take clear aim at your future.

I am a clinical psychologist with a private practice in New York City. My patients come from all walks of life. I was trained in a traditional model of clinical psychology. This foundation has helped me to understand and help the many wonderful people with whom I have had the opportunity to work over the years. Since beginning my training and practice, I have routinely integrated ideas and techniques from various disciplines, including

INTRODUCTION

improvisational theater, biology, sports, theology, martial arts, and the visual arts to inform my work and improve the well-being of my patients.

One of the great privileges of being a therapist is getting to know the intimate thoughts, feelings, and behaviors of people I might otherwise never meet or only get to know on a surface level. Being a confidant of so many fascinating souls has allowed me to understand the apparent pitfalls that we all struggle with from time to time and to develop strategies to see through the illusions that can hold us back. Having these types of relationships is special and illuminating in many ways, but one of the most powerful things I have come to appreciate is that beneath all our differences in terms of physical appearance, culture, ethnicity, wealth, and beliefs, we all have the same fundamental wishes for lives filled with play, purpose, and work.

Several years ago, while commuting back and forth to my office, I began jotting down notes about concepts and techniques that worked to help my patients take their next step. This book was born of those ideas and methods. I share this work with the hope that you will find it to be a useful guide wherever you are in your life. Whether you are just out of school, transitioning to a new career, or entering an active retirement, I hope that the concepts, exercises, and advice in this book will help you envision a horizon filled with possibility and move toward your next big thing with courage and conviction.

RUNNING
IN PLACE

Chapter

1

When people meet with me for the first time they never just come right out and say, "I'm stuck." Instead, what brings them into my office are symptoms of anxiety, depression, or difficulties in their relationships or at work. It is not uncommon for new patients to tell me that their lives feel empty, directionless, or even pointless. Some people will say that they feel detached from themselves, as though they are spectators—watching their lives and relationships unfold—observing, but not engaging in the action. These are all ways that different people express the sense that they are running in place—as if they are expending a lot of energy getting tired but not getting anywhere—that they are stuck in their own lives.

Why do they feel this way?

As we grow up and adapt to the challenges of life, we do what we have to do in order to survive. We work, get involved in relationships, and develop habits that help to keep us going. Yet many times—too many times—we get into situations or routines based on convenience rather than inspiration. We do what is easy instead of what is right for who we are and who we want to be. Instead of feeling charmed and excited by what lies ahead for us, we become experts at doing enough to get by. More and more of our time is spent putting Band-Aids on the things that just aren't working instead of re-examining, reimagining, and reshaping our lives based on what brings us meaning and joy. When we stop moving forward with a fresh vision for the future infused with passion and purpose, something fundamental inside of us dies. We become detached—absent from our own lives—and just a shadow remains. We'd rather be doing something else, even if we don't know what that something else is. One of my former patients, Rick, a partner at a law firm, explained it this way: "I hate my job, but it pays my kids' tuition. I do it and I do it well, but there is a part of me that is always working on my escape plan."

RUNNING IN PLACE? »

You may have noticed or sensed your friends, acquaintances, or coworkers running in place. Perhaps you've even thought or said something about it to yourself: "That guy is stuck!," "She seems so trapped," or "When is she going to move on with her life?" You may use different words to express it, but you can usually tell when someone else is running in place. My question is: Do you see it in yourself?

People can get stuck running in place in many different ways. I have had people come to meet with me because they feel trapped in a job, a relationship, a pattern of behavior, or a way of relating to the world.

If any of these sound like what you're going through, you're in the right place at the right time. This book is about discovering, imagining, and building your life so that it aligns with what brings you joy and gives you meaning. If you are not sure if, or how, you're running in place, let's start by looking at what I have found to be one of the most common areas of stagnation: your job. Here's a quiz that will help you determine if you're feeling stuck at work.

→ Go with Your Gut

When taking the quizzes in this book, answer the questions as quickly as you can. What we want here is just your gut reaction. Do not spend more than about ten seconds on any one question. If you are having a hard time deciding on an answer, put the book down for a few moments and pick it back up again when you are able to answer immediately, without deliberating too much. If you still find that you are having difficulty choosing an answer, the problem might be due to a conflict between how you feel and how you think you *should* feel. We will address this conflict in several places throughout the book, but especially in Chapter 5, when we meet your inner critic.

RUNNING IN PLACE AT WORK?

❶ Imagine that it is a typical Sunday night. Your weekend is winding down and you are about to go to bed. You set your alarm for the next morning and begin to think about the work week ahead. You feel ...

① At ease—you enjoy your weekends but you also get a lot out of your job, so you're fairly relaxed about starting the work week.

② A little bit down—you don't want to say goodbye to the weekend and your job may not be exactly what you want to be doing, but you don't dread going in there.

③ Sad or anxious—you hate your job and you don't know how you'll make it to Friday.

❷ Now imagine that you are actually at work. You are no busier or less busy than usual. You're just doing your thing. Take a moment to really plant yourself there. How do you feel?

① Engaged and stimulated.

② Indifferent.

③ Restless and distracted.

❸ Imagine that you are meeting someone for the first time. He asks you about your job. You describe what you do for a living. You are ...

① Talking excitedly about what you do.

② Describing your work in a detached way, almost as though you were talking about something that happened to a stranger.

③ Making excuses for why you do your job.

④ Now take a moment to think about a few of your coworkers with whom you interact on a regular basis. How do you see them?

① They are sources of inspiration and positive challenge.
② They are nice enough but nothing too special.
③ They seem dead inside.

⑤ Imagine that it is five years from now. You are still at your current job and things are pretty much the same. You have a bit more responsibility and you are making a little more money, but otherwise your days are much like they are now. How do you feel?

① Happy that you've been able to continue doing what you do.
② Comfortable enough, but not particularly interested or excited about what you're doing.
③ Desperate to get out of there to do anything else.

Congratulations! You have just finished your first quiz. By looking at how you might be feeling stuck at work you are already on the road to what's next for you. Let's see how you did. Add up your scores (1, 2, or 3) on the five questions from this quiz and look below to consider if and how you may be feeling stuck at your current job.

✚ ✚

Running in Place at Work?—Add It Up!

Total Score 5–7: You are not stuck! Keep on doing what you are doing. You have great positive momentum in your job. What's your secret?

Total Score 8–11: You are in a bit of a funk. You don't feel inspired by your job, but you are not totally stuck either. The exercises in this book can help you recapture your enthusiasm for your work life.

Total Score 12–15: You are running in place at your job. Keep reading. We're going to make some big changes together.

✚ ✚

The second most common area in which people tend to get stuck is in relationships. There are many different ways to stagnate in relationships. For example, you may be having difficulties getting into healthy romantic relationships or long-lasting, supportive friendships. Alternatively, you may feel trapped or confined because you routinely get into new relationships but can't seem to get out of them. Some people find that they look for new relationships yet they end up dating the same types of people over and over again—repeating old, unhealthy patterns from the past. Use this quiz to determine whether or not this is an area where you might need some help getting to your next big thing.

Quiz:

RUNNING IN PLACE
IN YOUR RELATIONSHIPS?

❶ **Imagine that it is a typical Saturday night. You have recovered from the week and are going out tonight. Who are you most likely to go out with? A spouse? A friend? A date? Picture this person in your mind. Now consider the night ahead. How do you feel?**

① You're enthusiastic about the time that you'll get to spend with this person.

② You're glad to be going out, but not particularly excited to be doing it with this person.

③ You're upset because you know exactly how tonight is going to go, and it's not going to go well.

❷ **Imagine for a moment that money is no object. You are about to plan a vacation to one of your favorite places on earth. You get to choose three people to go with you. How do you feel?**

① You're thrilled by this opportunity. You can't imagine spending this time with anyone but the three people you've chosen.

② You're happy to be going away, but not particularly excited about the company.

③ You're upset because you don't want to spend a lot of time with these people who might ruin the experience for you.

❸ Imagine that you are in an accident. You are not seriously hurt, but you will need help getting around for the next few weeks. Think for a moment about one person whom you will ask to help you out in your time of need. Picture this person well and then imagine actually asking them to help take care of you. How do you feel?

① You are confident and secure that the person you ask will be happy to be there for you.

② You're comfortable asking because you know you need help, but you're also a bit worried about putting the other person out.

③ You're deeply uncomfortable about asking anyone to help you.

Now add up your scores (1, 2, or 3) on the three relationship questions and look below to find out if you are running in place in your personal relationships.

✦ ✦

Running in Place in Your Relationships?—Add It Up!

Total Score 3–4: Onward and upward! You are comfortable, confident, and secure with your closest relationships. The people around you are wonderful sources of support, inspiration, and intimacy.

Total Score 5–6: Meh. You have some good people around you. You may not feel inspired by your close relationships, but they add to your life and are a source of comfort to you. The exercises in this book will help you deepen your relationships or create new ones in order to get the most out of life.

Total Score 7–9: You're running in place. Your closest relationships are either stale or their bonds of trust or intimacy have been frayed. First, we will help you understand why you're in this situation; then we will get you moving on to what's next for you.

✦ ✦

As I mentioned before, people can get stuck in all sorts of ways—work and relationships are just two of the most common. People have come to me because they feel like they are running in place in their creative lives, trapped by feelings or behavior patterns from the past, or confined by old ways of seeing themselves and their possibilities for the future.

Take some time now to consider other areas of your life where you just can't seem to get much traction. Think about the barriers that you feel are in your way. We will deal with these in time. You can write some of these down. In fact, you may want to keep a journal with you as we go. This will give you a place to write down your answers to the exercises and jot down inspirations or new possibilities for yourself. It may be helpful to refer back to them along the journey from running in place to moving with purpose.

For some people, running in place is a lifestyle. They are moving, of course, because they need to keep food on the table and a roof over their heads. However, they can't seem to take action on what's next because they don't see a way out of their situation. This was certainly the case for a woman named Amanda with whom I worked several years ago.

⫸⫸⫸ Amanda ⫷⫷⫷

Amanda was depressed.

Forty-one years old and single with one child, she was working full time as an administrative assistant at a law firm. She hated her job, which she described as "soul-crushing" and besides her daughter Hannah, the one light in her life, nothing felt right.

After Amanda got home from work she typically fixed a meal, put Hannah to bed, grabbed the remote control and a glass of Chardonnay, and collapsed onto her couch. At least two nights a week—though more often three or four—she passed out in front of the TV. Amanda had put on weight and felt awful about the person she had become. She knew that things couldn't go on the way they were, but she had no idea what to do next.

Amanda knew she wasn't living. She just didn't know how to change. Something was wrong, but she couldn't say exactly what it was. Instead, Amanda said she was stuck in other ways: She was often sad, irritable, angry, fatigued, and indecisive. She was twenty pounds heavier than she had been barely five years before. Amanda couldn't sleep, concentrate, or enjoy herself. She procrastinated about everything.

This kind of running in place is quite common. It wasn't over the top or obvious to the people around her, but in some ways it was more insidious. Amanda was stuck because she couldn't envision her life being any different. She was stagnant. To her, life felt long and painful; it was a dull, throbbing ache that she carried with her wherever she went. Her work seemed to take up all her time and drain away her energy. Collapsing on the couch with a remote control in one hand and a glass of wine in the other was the only way she could cope.

Amanda was running in place because she couldn't move out of a repetitive pattern of behavior; it didn't feel right to her, but she couldn't stop.

Does anything in Amanda's story sound or feel familiar? Does it reflect aspects of your own experience?

To determine whether you are stuck in the same way as Amanda, consider the following questions.

Quiz:

RUNNING IN PLACE AS A LIFESTYLE?

❶ How often do you try to do something new and different?

① Every day—that's the best way to squeeze the most juice out of life.

② Once in a while—just so life doesn't get too repetitive and boring.

③ Rarely—who has the time, energy, or interest for anything new or different?

❷ Do you set goals for yourself and work hard to achieve them?

① Yes—you're a goal-setting and -accomplishing machine. Rarrh!

② Sort of—you do set goals for yourself but tend to give up when things get tough.

③ No—you don't set goals to achieve because you're afraid you'll fail.

③ **When problems spring up in your life, how do you typically deal with them?**

① You attack them with controlled fury.

② You procrastinate until there is no other choice but to deal with them.

③ You try to avoid them and pray they will go away.

Add up your scores (1, 2, or 3) on the three lifestyle questions and look below to learn whether or not you are running in place in other parts of your life.

✚ ✚

Running in Place as a Lifestyle?—Add It Up!

Total Score 3–4: You have fire and fury and are charging forward. Go you!

Total Score 5–6: You are not exactly running in place, but you don't have much forward momentum either. You get things done when you have to, but tend to procrastinate or wait until you have no other choice. Keep reading. We are going to help propel you forward with a few strategies and techniques.

Total Score 7–9: You are running in place, but that is about to end. Together we will help you find your purpose and take action on your next big thing.

✚ ✚

Perhaps my patient Amanda was so focused on just getting through each day and making ends meet that she never looked up to consider where she might go or how life could be different. This was a problem for her, but one that we were able to address through some exercises aimed at helping her reimagine her life. If you're in a similar situation, we will ignite your vision together with the exercises in Chapter 3. Having a vision is a key for getting to your next big thing. Use the following quiz to consider if you are having difficulties imagining a new horizon.

Quiz:

RUNNING WITH VISION?

❶ When you think about your life in five years, what do you imagine it will be like?

① It will be vastly different, probably in a good way.
② It will be about the same as it is now.
③ It will be worse—it's frightening to even consider it.

❷ How much time do you spend imagining new horizons?

① A lot. You're constantly dreaming up new ways of living and envisioning new and exciting possibilities for the future.
② Some. You think about different possibilities for yourself, but it's not a big focus in your mind.
③ None. Change is rare and rarely good.

❸ Think back five years. Did you envision and work to create the life you have today?

① Yes. You planned it all and it worked out almost exactly as you had hoped.
② Sort of. You had a vague idea of how your life would be now. There are some parts of it that worked out as you planned and some that didn't.
③ You didn't plan anything. It all just sort of happened.

Add up your scores (1, 2, or 3) on the three vision questions, and look below to consider how much you use your imagination to fuel your vision.

Running with Vision?—Add It Up!

Total Score 3–4: You are an imaginative soul. Keep on dreaming and moving forward toward your dreams.

Total Score 5–6: Your imagination is your friend, but we need to pump it up and get you dreaming bigger and living larger.

Total Score 7–9: We need to get you imagining again. You still have it. We all do; we just need to restart your creative mind to get you unstuck.

MOVING WITH PURPOSE »

What I've outlined above are several different ways that you may be running in place. Maybe one of them applies to your situation. Perhaps you've discovered that you're stuck in more than one way or in a way we haven't yet discussed. In any case, what's more important than how you are running in place is how we are going to get you moving with purpose. Well, buckle up and buckle down, because you're about to find out.

PLAY, PURPOSE, AND WORK »

Obviously, my approach to working with each of my patients is different depending on the person's particular needs and situation. However, I have found that regardless of *how* my patients may feel stuck when they first enter my office, there are three key elements for getting them moving on to what's next in their lives. These are: play, purpose, and work. As we travel down this road of getting you to your next big thing, you will reconnect with your innate sense of play so you can discover your personal purpose, and work toward a better future. The reasons that play, purpose, and work are so critical for getting to what's next are:

- **Play**—Reconnecting with your imagination and innate sense of play will help you envision a new horizon for yourself.

- **Purpose**—Discovering your personal purpose will help you decide what you need to do in order to have a meaningful life.
- **Work**—The effort and energy you put toward your vision for what's next will make it a reality.

≫ Play

Although we are all born with different ways of playing, something we will talk about more in Chapter 3, play and imagination are not just for kids. Play is a way of experiencing and exploring the world. When you play you are present; you're in the Now. Although you may learn and accomplish a lot during play, you do not play in order to learn or accomplish. You play in order to play. Playing is being.

When you play, your mind and imagination are open to thoughts you have never had before. Playing allows you to experiment with new ways of living. It is a natural and instinctive process—if you are looking at this with a suspicious eye right now, I'm talking to you. Play and imagination are vital to getting to your next big thing. You must play with, and explore, ideas before you craft your new vision for your future. If it's been a while since you played, you may have forgotten how; we'll get there. But if you are like most of the people I speak to, I might need to convince you first about the importance of play.

≫ Purpose

Purpose is your way of making sense of your place in the world. We will talk a lot about your purpose throughout this book, especially in Chapter 4. But for now, let's briefly touch on what purpose is.

Purpose is a choice.

Whether we think about it or ignore it, every single one of us makes a profound choice that ultimately shapes our paths. We can choose to believe that our lives are part of a larger plan or that they are random and trivial. We may have faith that there is a given path for each of us, or we may feel that we are just here by luck or chance and there is no grand scheme to guide our lives.

As a therapist who has worked with many people struggling to find purpose in their lives, I can tell you this: Those who seek reasons for their existence will find them, and those who don't, won't. But whether you believe in a larger plan for your life or think that such an idea is nonsense, to move forward you must have, find, or create a personal sense of purpose.

Purpose comes down to a choice: If you can imagine, or believe in, a reason for your life and choose to let your understanding guide your actions, then by definition you are living a life of purpose.

» Work

Finally, of course, there's work. When you are living with play and purpose, work is a good thing. Really. Work puts your play and purpose into practice.

Work is how you are going to get to your next big thing. By putting your energy into what you believe, you can embody the vision that you imagined and live a life of purpose. Working toward what's next may not be like work you've done in the past. If you are doing a job where you're working for someone else, your tasks are often laid out in front of you. You have obvious successes or failures along the way for you and others to see. When you are working toward your next big thing, you are working for *you*. You are the boss—you get the grime and the glory.

Your Next Big Thing is about recasting your life so that it aligns with what is important to you. These three elements—play, purpose, and work—are the basis of the ten steps in this book, which will help you know who you are, imagine what you can be, and move with purpose toward your vision.

This book, and the ten steps you will take along the way, are divided into three parts.

In the first part, you will get to know yourself by exploring your imagination and connecting with your purpose.

In the second part, you will begin to take action on your vision through making time for yourself and learning how to transform your obstacles into opportunities. You will then come face to face with your inner critic—the voice inside of you that tries to keep you safe but confined. You will push past the three-headed monster of Passivity, Procrastination, and Perfectionism, which will try to keep you from moving forward.

In the third part, you will release the hero that has been waiting inside of you all along. You will learn to live in the Now and share what you have learned along the way.

These ten steps are the way to get from the Now You to the New You. Each step will help you build on the last so that you can move forward in a way that honors your personal process and brings you into a new chapter of your life with confidence in yourself and faith in your future.

Here is an overview of the ten steps we will take together.

» STEP 1. Know Yourself.

You will start your journey by taking stock of where you are in your life and considering how you got here. We will learn about your roles, your values, and what brings you joy. After all, you must know who you are before you can know where you want to go.

» STEP 2. Imagine Yourself.

In this step you will rediscover your innate sense of play and learn how to use your imagination to envision a new horizon.

» STEP 3. Discover Your Purpose.

Here we will connect you with your core values in order to develop a personal Statement of Purpose. Once you know what is truly important to you, your next big thing is often just a matter of taking action.

» STEP 4. Face Your Inner Critic.

As you envision a new life for yourself, the voice inside of you that wants to hold you back will undoubtedly emerge. We will learn where this voice comes from and how to face it in order to move forward.

» STEP 5. Take Action.

This step is about getting over the initial barriers to action. You will learn several techniques to overcome inertia and create the time you need in order to get you moving.

» STEP 6. Embrace Your Process.

Here you will learn how to see your path as a process. You will find that bends in the road are not the end of the road but opportunities that are actually invaluable for your journey.

» STEP 7. Defeat the Three-Headed Monster.

In this step you will confront the three-headed monster of Passivity, Procrastination, and Perfectionism in order to persist on your journey and come through on the other side.

» STEP 8. Reclaim Your Inner Hero.

Here you will learn to value yourself in order to put you back at the center of your own life.

» STEP 9. Live in the Now.

You will discover that the secret to getting to your next big thing is living in the Now. You will learn exactly what this phrase means, why it is essential, and how to do it.

» STEP 10. Share Yourself.

As you move toward your new life, you will naturally begin to connect your process with the journeys of other people. You will learn why, how, and when to share yourself with those around you. And, perhaps more important, when not to share.

As you go through these steps, your vision for yourself will widen. You will see a path to a new future and take decisive action to make that vision a reality. These steps are the key to getting you from running in place to moving with purpose toward your next big thing.

We are going to start our journey at the beginning—I know that may seem obvious, but it's not (more on this in Chapter 6). To get to the New You, we will start with the Now You. Every journey begins with a step. Ours begins by getting to know who you are now and how you got here.

Let's get to it!

THE TAKEAWAY

1 Running in place results from getting into jobs, relationships, or habits based on convenience rather than inspiration. When this happens there are parts of us that get left behind.

2 You can be stuck in several ways including your career, your relationships, and your ways of behaving and relating to the world.

3 In order to decide and take action on what's next, you need three things: play, purpose, and work.

4 Play helps you imagine what you want, purpose helps you decide what you need, and work gets you there.

5 The journey from running in place to moving with purpose involves ten steps:

Step 1. Know Yourself
Step 2. Imagine Yourself
Step 3. Discover Your Purpose
Step 4. Face Your Inner Critic
Step 5. Take Action
Step 6. Embrace Your Process

Step 7. Defeat the Three-Headed Monster
Step 8. Reclaim Your Inner Hero
Step 9. Live in the Now
Step 10. Share Yourself

PART

1

Knowing Your Path

KNOW YOURSELF

Chapter

2

When you feel stuck, personally or professionally, the first thing to do is regroup—take stock of who you are, where you are, and how you got here. This is where we will begin our journey together. Before we envision what's next for you, we need to understand what's now. The Now You is the foundation for the New You, so we'd better get to know the Now You very well. By learning about yourself inside and out you will come to appreciate what you want to change and what you don't. No matter how many important people you have in your life who will be a part of your future, *you* are the catalyst for change in your life—it all starts with you.

Speaking of you, who are you, anyway?

WHO ARE YOU? »

In order to get to know you, we are going to go from the outside in. In this chapter we are going to look at the Now You in three different ways. First, we will learn about the roles you currently play, then we are going to define your values, and finally we will spend some time helping you to discover what brings you joy. Just so we are clear, let's define what these three things are:

- **Roles:** what you do
- **Values:** what's important to you
- **Joy:** when what you do and what's important to you are aligned

When you know the roles you play, the values you hold, and what brings you joy, you can very quickly come to see what you want your life to be. We will start by getting to know your roles so that you can assess which ones are working for you and which ones are not. We will uncover your values because you need to own what's important to you in order to live a life of purpose. Finally, we are going to learn about what brings you joy, because if you are not engaging with Activities of Joy, life is just another task that you have to do instead of an unfinished adventure that you *get* to do.

So come on, let's get to know you.

ROLES »

Let's pretend that you don't know anything about yourself and that you are meeting you for the first time. By looking at the various roles you play we will get to see clearly how the outside world makes sense of you.

As we grow and develop we tend to label ourselves. Having labels or roles to define who we are is useful.

- There are relationship roles, like son, brother, friend, partner, or granddaughter.
- There are job roles, like teacher, administrator, or nurse.
- There are group roles that may include ethnic, religious, cultural, or subcultural groups.

The list of the types of roles we play can be practically endless.

Knowing our roles helps us to know ourselves. This is particularly useful during tough times. When we feel unsettled by the changes that life brings, having knowledge about our place in the world can feel reassuring.

Although some of our roles can help us feel steady during turbulent times, others can hold us back. *Knowing* what we are is very different from *imagining* who or what we can be. Because your roles have the potential to keep you stuck, you need to get to know them, and know them well.

Whenever there is something or somebody in your way, the best approach is to first learn as much about them as possible and then get close to them. We will talk more about this strategy in Chapter 5, when we meet your inner critic.

Let's make a list of the roles you currently play.

When someone meets you for the first time and is trying to get to know you, they typically ask questions about the roles that you perform or groups you belong to.

Here are some examples of the types of roles you might use to describe yourself to other people:

- → secretary
- → mother
- → intellectual
- → liberal
- → Christian
- → husband
- → lawyer
- → bacon lover
- → Canadian
- → romantic
- → Cheesehead
- → conservative
- → actor
- → coffee drinker
- → golfer
- → vegan
- → father of three
- → scout leader
- → dentist
- → waiter
- → Libertarian
- → Red Sox fan

Exercise:

WHAT ARE YOUR ROLES?

What roles would you use to describe yourself when meeting someone for the first time?

Take out a notebook or a piece of paper, or call up a blank document on your computer and make two columns. Leave the right column blank. In the left column, write down a list of no more than ten roles that you currently play. Please write down any roles that you feel define who you are. You may want to include relationship or family roles (e.g., mother, daughter, husband), job roles (e.g., part-time tutor, part-time caretaker), group roles (e.g., Republican, Democrat, Yankee), or any roles that you feel help to describe who you are to the outside world. There are no right answers—just the answers that best describe you now. Please keep the list to ten roles or less. You might be able to go on and on, but ten should allow you to get to the essence of the roles that you currently play.

Here is a sample of what your list from this exercise might look like:

CURRENT ROLES	
Mother of five	
Nurse	
Wife	
Episcopalian	
Grandmother	
Caretaker	
Collage maker	
Red Sox fan	
Pet owner	
PTA president	

Soak in your answers. Own what you wrote. Your responses to these questions are important because they are how the world sees you now.

Now that we know what your roles are, let's take some time to consider how you feel you are doing in your roles. Let's sort out what roles you feel you are doing well in, which ones can use a little improvement, and which ones need to be changed. It's important to know that some roles that you play are permanent and can never be altered (e.g., mother, Red Sox fan), others may be modified with a little effort (e.g., vegan, golfer, Libertarian), and still others may be changed only with considerable struggle or pain (e.g., bacon lover, aspiring writer).

Exercise:

PERFORMING YOUR ROLES

Look at the list of roles that you wrote down in the left column, and in the right column write down one of three things: "Doing great," "Needs improvement," or "Must change." Here's an example of what this might look like:

CURRENT ROLES	STATUS
Mother of five	Doing great
Nurse	Must change
Wife	Needs improvement
Episcopalian	Needs improvement
Grandmother	Doing great
Caretaker	Needs improvement
Collage maker	Must change
Red Sox fan	Doing great
Pet owner	Doing great
PTA president	Needs improvement

Thinking through your current roles may also help you to consider roles you would like to have. If you found yourself doing this, please take a moment now to make a list of "aspirational roles" (roles you would like to play). We will come back to these in Chapter 4 when we help to connect you with your personal purpose.

Now that you have a good sense of your roles, which ones you feel are going smoothly, and which ones could use some improvement or changing, let's turn our attention to other matters related to who you are now. In the next section we are going to focus on what *matters* to you: your values.

VALUES »

Your values, simply put, are whatever is important to you. Everyone has values. They come from our parents, our cultures, our society, our biology, our personal history, and our joys. Some examples of values are freedom, happiness, spirituality, enlightenment, and family, though there are dozens of others.

What are your values? Values can, and do, change over time, but our goal in this chapter is to get to know the Now You, so as you do this next exercise, please try to stay centered in the Now. I only want you to consider your current values—not your values from yesterday, last month, or fifteen years from now. With that in mind, please complete the following exercise:

Exercise:

WHAT ARE YOUR VALUES?

Look at the following list of values and mark off which ones are essential to you. Once you've had a chance to soak these in, choose the three you feel are most important to you. We will call these three your core values. After you have selected them you can write them down in your journal, on your own paper, or in the center circle below. It may be hard to choose because you have more than three values, but you will have a chance to add more values shortly and you can always reorder them later if need be. This list is extensive enough that it should contain at least some of your personal values, but if there is a value you hold dear that is not on the list, feel free to add it.

1. Adventure
2. Balance
3. Beauty
4. Being inspired
5. Caring for others
6. Caring for myself
7. Charity
8. Comfort
9. Connection
10. Creative expression
11. Ease
12. Education
13. Enlightenment
14. Excitement
15. Exploration
16. Faith
17. Fame
18. Family
19. Freedom
20. Friendship
21. Happiness

22. Health
23. Inspiring others
24. Justice
25. Knowledge
26. Laughter
27. Leaving a legacy
28. Marriage
29. Peace
30. Personal fulfillment
31. Personal power
32. Physical pleasure
33. Physical power
34. Reduction of suffering
35. Religion
36. Romantic love
37. Security
38. Self-expression
39. Spirituality
40. Wealth
41. Wisdom
42. Working hard

Now that you have had a chance to look over the list, it's time to make some choices. Put your top three core values in the center circle below:

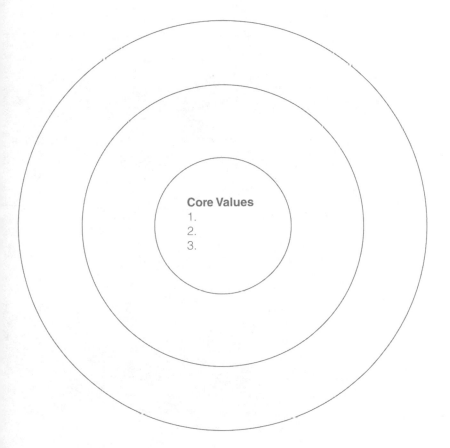

Core Values
1.
2.
3.

Choose your three next most important values, which we will call your secondary values, and put them in the second circle, like this:

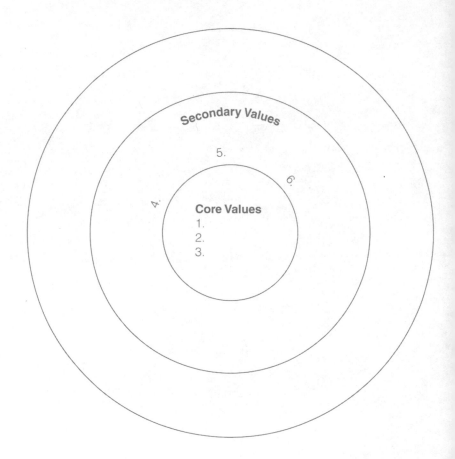

Finally, choose the four next most important values to you, which we will call your ancillary values and place them in the outer circle, like this:

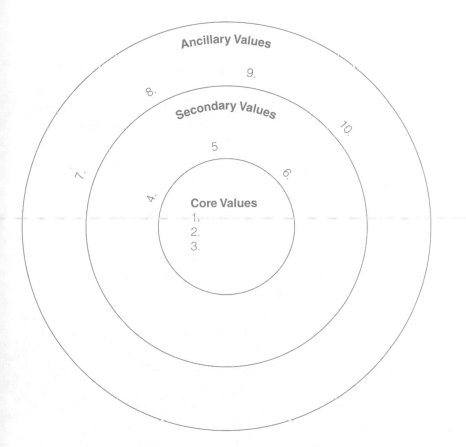

Look over the values you chose. Now take a moment to give yourself credit for doing this exercise. It can be difficult, but once you know your values you are well on your way to discovering your next big thing. We are going to come back to your diagram several times throughout the book, and it will be especially important as we consider your personal purpose in Chapter 4, so you may want to keep it handy.

Okay, now that you know what you do with your time (roles) and what's important to you (values), we need to focus on what happens when what you do and what matters to you come together. We need to know what brings you joy.

WHAT IS JOY? »

Many people think of joy as happiness, and the two are closely linked, but they are not the same thing. Happiness is great, but joy is more than that. When you are engaged in an Activity of Joy you are in the moment—totally present. You are consumed—in a state where time has no meaning and all that exists is Now. Your joy is your guide. When you are living in joy your life flows. Opportunities and experiences that you may have never dreamed of come your way. You are engaged, excited, and, well . . . joyful.

If you are feeling stuck you may not spend much time focused on joy these days, but that's going to change.

» Joy

Discovering or rediscovering what brings you joy is a critical part of figuring out your next big thing, because sometimes once you have a firm grasp on what makes your life flow, what you want to do next may become crystal clear. If you are not sure what brings you joy, or you think that nothing brings you joy, I can assure you that *everyone* has things that bring them joy. It may just be a matter of looking for yours.

In order to discover what brings you joy we are going to start with the Now You and work our way back to the Then You.

What brings you joy is personal. Take a moment now to think about things that you do or have been doing for the past five years that you enjoy. You may consider different things that you do with your time that make you happy, including hobbies. We are going to look at these carefully to see if they are Activities of Joy.

Pick one of these activities and keep it in mind as you do the following quiz.

WHAT ARE YOUR ACTIVITIES OF JOY?

❶ When you do this activity do you feel engaged, stimulated, or excited?

① Yes. When you're doing this you're like a dog with a bone.

② Meh. It raises your blood pressure but you'd just as soon be watching reruns of *Seinfeld*.

③ No. There are many other things you'd rather be doing than this.

❷ Do you feel challenged or look for new challenges when doing this activity?

① Yes. You are always looking for new ways to push yourself to grow, learn, and develop when doing this activity.

② Sort of. You do it mainly because it is easy or comes naturally to you.

③ No. If you do it at all, you just want to get through it.

❸ What does time feel like when you are doing this activity?

① You don't even notice the time when you're engaged in it.

② Neither faster nor slower than usual.

③ As slowly as if you were doing your taxes (no offense to the accountants out there).

❹ Would you do this activity even if you didn't have to?

① Absolutely. If you didn't have to work or shower, you could do this practically 24–7.

② Maybe. You do enjoy it but if you didn't have to do it, you might not.

③ They couldn't pay you enough to do it.

Now add up the scores (1, 2, or 3) on these three questions, and look below to discover if you have found an Activity of Joy.

What Are Your Activities of Joy?—Add It Up!

Total Score 4–6: Yeah! Joy to the world.

Total Score 7–9: Not exactly. What you have may be something that makes you happy or distracts you from unpleasantness. We will find your joy; we just need to look a little harder.

Total Score 10–12: Not by a long shot. This is not an Activity of Joy. In fact, you may want to consider not doing this activity at all. We may need you to dig into your past to unearth your joy.

+ + + + + + + + + + + + + + + + + + + +

If you found an Activity of Joy through this quiz, I can assure you of two things: First, you know something very important about yourself that will be critical as you take the next steps on your journey. Second, the fact that you have maintained this Activity of Joy up to this point in your life means that even if you are feeling stuck, your compass is pointing in the right direction.

If you did not identify an Activity of Joy, do not fret. First, try using another current activity that you think might be an Activity of Joy and use the quiz again to see if it is. If that does not work, again, do not despair. There is joy for you too— it just might not be at the top of your mind because you haven't done it in a while.

Search through activities from your past. If you flip back a bit into your history, your joy is somewhere in there, even if it's not immediately obvious to you because it may not be part of your life right now. This is not uncommon.

When you finish school or training and go out into the world, you are faced with greater demands on your time and energy, which are two of your most valuable commodities. During the process of adapting to the grown-up world, activities that were once a major part of your life in childhood or adolescence fall by the wayside so that you can fulfill the practical demands of daily life. This development is part of the transition to the working years. Pruning "excess" activities makes good sense and is necessary to some degree, but often we shear too closely in the name of efficiency. We discard the very activities that we should keep. For example, suppose dancing or singing was an Activity of Joy in the past. You may not spend much time doing those things now, and as a result you feel an emptiness in your life, even if you're not sure why. By letting go of some favored activities we often forget about what brings us joy. These activities are essential for understanding and guiding our lives. When you understand what brings you joy, your next big thing tends to flow naturally.

Exercise:

PAST ACTIVITIES OF JOY

Think for a moment about when you were younger. Were there any activities that just seemed to come easier to you than to other people? Was there something that you gravitated toward that just felt right? Did you like to sketch, paint, or make collages? Were you an athlete or an actor? A master of Legos or Erector sets? Did you perform comedy, make movies, or write short stories? Was there any activity that you could do for hours on end? Did time move more quickly when you were singing, knitting, or designing a video game? When you had free time did you instinctively build, sew, draw, play music, write, dance, sing, or bake? Perhaps there were a few activities that came naturally to you.

When you have one or more of these activities from your past in mind, try taking the Activities of Joy quiz previously in order to determine if this is in fact a true Activity of Joy or something else.

Several patients have asked me why they have gravitated toward these Activities of Joy. I don't have the answer to that question, but I actually don't think "why" really matters. There is something inside of us that just knows things that we may not have the words to explain. We each have a natural voice within us that, if we listen to it, brings us to where we need to be. Whether you call it instinct, intuition, or any other name, each of us is born with a way of expressing ourselves that just feels right. Unfortunately, most of us are taught not to listen to this guide. As you come to know and walk your path, that long-silenced voice will begin to light your way and help you decide and take action on what's next for you.

» Leading with Joy

Ignoring what brings you joy often pushes you into dead ends. On the other hand, allowing Activities of Joy to lead can bring you to new horizons you might not have imagined before. Using your joy helps you make better choices that are in line with your values and purpose. When you are in sync with your priorities your life becomes full, even magical. Regardless of whether you are stuck in a job, a dysfunctional relationship, or a pattern of behavior that's just not working for you, having and knowing your joy helps give you definition. It reminds you of who you are and what's important to you.

Take a moment and appreciate what you are doing here. If you have done all of these exercises, you know a lot more about yourself than you did when you started this chapter. You know what roles you play and how you feel about those roles; you know what brings you joy; and you know what your values are. You are on the road to your next big thing!

If you had some difficulty working through these exercises, don't be discouraged. When you feel stuck in a job, a relationship, or a way of life, the world can seem cruel and unforgiving. It's at these times that we most want to distract ourselves, shut it all out, or hide. While this might feel good in the short term, in the long run the reasons you got stuck in the first place are still there. It's up to you to remake your life into the one you want. You can do it, and getting to know yourself is the first step of your journey. This can be hard, and it can feel particularly intimidating if you are running in place. Consider how difficult this was for one man with whom I worked a few years ago, named Chuck.

 Chuck

Chuck was a thirty-nine-year-old, single man who had recently broken up with a woman. He came to meet with me because he got into a fistfight with a colleague outside of a bar over a $20 bet on an Ohio State basketball game while they were watching the annual NCAA tournament. As it turns out, his colleague was a former patient of mine. On the Monday after the fight, Chuck's colleague strongly encouraged him to meet with me.

Chuck worked for a large, well-known bank, and from a financial point of view he was quite successful. Yet from the moment I met him I could feel how angry he was. Less than ten minutes into our first session he told me that he often yelled at people who moved too slowly in front of him in line or who inadvertently blocked his path on the sidewalk. He was a loose cannon, and I was immediately concerned about his potential for violence.

Getting to know Chuck was hard for me, but it was even harder for him. It is not uncommon that when someone has been deeply scarred, the walls that they put up to defend themselves from further pain can feel almost impossible to scale. That was the case with Chuck.

Chuck resisted my questions about the roles he played and lobbed some obscenities in my direction when I asked him to consider Activities of Joy.

He was in my office, which meant that he wanted to change; but like many people, Chuck needed some time to get to know himself. He wasn't yet ready to examine himself from the outside in, so we started where he was more comfortable: by looking at his values.

Although you may not have as violent a reaction to this exercise as Chuck did, seeing how difficult this was for him can help you appreciate the steep challenges of getting to know yourself. It doesn't matter exactly where you start the process, only that you do so honestly, and that you do so—period. You should go about it in your own way and in your own time. There is no single, absolute formula for change. You will discover the ingredients that I have found to be helpful throughout this book, but exactly how and when you do it is up to you. We are working toward real, meaningful, and sustainable change for you, so it is critical to start from where you are rather than where you want to be or where you, or others, think you *should* be. In fact, I have found that when you try to start too far ahead of where you are, change can feel particularly daunting. We'll get there.

Change is hard, and you will have moments of doubt on your path; we all do from time to time. But if you know yourself and value who you are, you will have the strength to move through the fear.

Regardless of how many of these exercises you did, just beginning to think about change is a big step, because it's the first step. You have taken it. You are here. Now that we have a better picture of who you are, we can begin to imagine where you want to go. On to Step Two, where you will use your imagination to open yourself up to a new vision of who you can be.

THE
TAKEAWAY

1 You worked on grounding yourself in the present by getting to know yourself from the outside in.

2 You considered the types of roles you currently play and your personal values.

3 You investigated your Activities of Joy from the present and the past.

IMAGINE YOURSELF

Chapter

3

When you've been running in place in one or more areas of your life—whether it's in a job situation, a relationship, or a pattern of behavior—it is natural to narrow your focus and energy in order to get by or get through. The problem is that getting by and getting through have nothing to do with getting better. That is what this chapter is all about: imagining something better.

You have already taken your first step of the journey. You have knowledge. You know yourself—your roles, your values, and what brings you joy. Now we need to know where you are going. So grab a bag, pack your imagination, and let's play.

PLAY »

You may be wondering why you need play and imagination on your journey, but the fact of the matter is, these are the tools you've always used to help you grow, even if you didn't realize it.

Consider for a moment what it is like to be a child. Children get stuck in their lives all the time when they bump up against experiences or ideas that are beyond their capacity to comprehend. As they grow and develop, all children must come to terms with feeling vulnerable and scared from time to time. Very young children need to make sense of intense concepts such as pain, loss, and, unfortunately, at times even trauma and death. The gap between kids' experiences and understanding can be quite large. Children need a way to take in new and frightening experiences or they would constantly feel overwhelmed. Without some tool for helping them get unstuck, children would spend their lives in fear of what they don't— and can't—understand.

Fortunately, conveniently, all children are born with just such a tool.

That tool . . .

Wait for it . . .

Wait for it . . .

. . . is play.

›› What Play Is Not

What exactly is play? And how does it help get you to your next big thing? Let's start by talking about what play is not. This is probably obvious, but play is not work. Work is future focused. It is about achieving goals. When you are working, all of your energy is directed toward the distance. You solve, build, and plan for later. You aim at a specific target, something to achieve in the future. Success at work requires consistency, effort, and endurance. Working is doing.

So what about play? Unfortunately, most adults think of play as something that's just for children, and it often is—though it should not be.

Play is an essential part of life at every age. It is a way of experiencing and exploring the world that allows you to open your mind to fresh ideas and experiment with new ways of being. It is about process and exploration rather than goals and achievement. Imaginative play is open-ended. It does not follow a linear path. There is no correct way to play (though there are some ways to play that are better than others, but more on that later), no right answer, no beginning, and no end. It is exploration without judgment and consequence. Playing is being.

Here is a side-by-side comparison of work and play:

WORK VERSUS PLAY	
Work	Play
Future focused	Present focused
Goal oriented	Process oriented
Binary	Unfinished
Linear	Nonlinear
Success or failure	Open-ended

What is amazing about play is that it requires so little yet gives us so much. Plus it's fun! Although play is not necessarily about achieving specific objectives, you actually accomplish a lot through imagination and play. Playing in your mind allows you to come to terms with the past and forge ahead into the future through being in the present. It is your natural stimulator and simulator. Plus, without it, none of us would even make it to adulthood.

Without play we wouldn't be able to open our minds to concepts that would otherwise be too much to handle. Play allows us to try out different ways of understanding new and frightening situations without experiencing our terror head-on. By using our imaginations and playing out different scenarios, our minds run through various possibilities and outcomes so that we can teach ourselves how we might handle them. Play is a natural form of problem solving that gives us the chance to make sense of the world and our roles in it by letting us try out new identities, strategies, and possibilities for how to move ahead. It gives us access to ideas that never existed before, allows us to experience the world in a safe way, and helps us envision our horizons with less fear and more faith. It is these aspects of play that make it a critical step toward your next big thing.

» What Can Play Do for Me?

Let's begin by understanding what Play has already done for you. Then we will come to how Play can help you now. Imagine (or remember), for example, that you are three years old and you suddenly find out that your parents will be having a new baby—a boy. They are delighted and hope that you will be too. It sort of sounds okay, but you're just not sure. I mean, let's face it: You are *it*. You have either been the only one, or one of the only ones, your whole life—and now suddenly there will be someone else taking attention from Mommy and Daddy.

Perhaps you think: "There's only one room and one crib. Where will he sleep? Wait, where will I sleep? He's not going to take Bunny away! Will he? Can he? Why is this happening to me?"

Your whole world is about to change. Are you ready for it? How do you make sense of this? What could you do to come to terms with the unthinkable unknown? How could you possibly understand it and still carry on?

You do it the way we all do it: with play and imagination. You try out different possible scenarios and roles in your mind and in your play. You might take the role of the little brother or the caregiver, or you might play yourself in the drama. Whatever you do, make no mistake about it: You play.

That is how you moved forward as a child, and that's exactly how you are going to do it now.

To get to your next big thing, you need to use imaginative play in order to get through your feelings of stuckness so that you can dream up the future that you want. Playing with ideas allows you to imagine a new future so that you can begin moving forward. Working gets you there. Combining the working you with the playing you is a centering experience because there is more of you here in the present. You are working toward the New while you are playing in the Now.

IMAGINE »

Play and imagination are imperative for our development throughout our lives. Yet even people who idealize imagination and creative play as important values to instill in their children are often willing to ignore it in their own lives. I've met people who wouldn't send their kids to a school that lacked an arts program, yet they never even consider that they themselves should be spending time playing and imagining. How does something that is so vital at one point in life suddenly become irrelevant at another? If we value play and imagination in the early years because they promote healthy minds and contribute to a strong sense of self, why are they not an essential part of adulthood? Do we not need an outlet for self-expression or a sense of emotional well-being as adults?

Actually, we do.

What about you? Do you play? Take the following quiz and find out.

Quiz:

DO YOU PLAY?

❶ Do you consider yourself a playful person?

① Absolutely. Playing is essential to living.

② Kind of. You would like to play more but sometimes you have a hard time letting go.

③ No way. Play is for kids. You're not a kid and you don't feel comfortable playing as an adult.

② Do you consider your imagination to be an important part of who you are?

① Yes. You're constantly dreaming up new ideas for your future and imagining exciting new horizons.

② Sort of. You're a practical person and so you spend most of your mindshare on reality, but occasionally you imagine or daydream about a brighter future.

③ No. Who has time for imagination?

③ When do you play?

① Often. You try to bring your sense of play to almost everything you do. If you take life too seriously it gets boring.

② Every once in a while, with a small number of trusted people.

③ You never play these days.

Add up the scores (1, 2, or 3) on the three questions and look below to learn how playful you are these days.

✚ ✚

Do You Play?—Add It Up!

Total Score 3–4: You are an imaginative soul. Keep on dreaming and moving forward toward your dreams.

Total Score 5–6: Your imagination is your friend, but we need to pump it up and get you dreaming bigger and living larger.

Total Score 7–9: We need to get you imagining again. You still have it. We all do; we just need to restart your creative mind to get you unstuck.

✚ ✚

I hope that your answers to this quiz helped to give you a sense of how much you play. Play and imagination are essential in order for you to envision a new horizon and ultimately to get to what's next. Even if the

Now You hasn't been playing much these days, do not worry, because the New You will. You know how to play, even if it's been a while. It doesn't matter how playful you have been, just how playful you are willing to be. Before we move on to discussing how to use play and imagination to move beyond running in place to moving with purpose, let's consider what has been getting in the way of play for you.

Quiz:

WHAT'S IN THE WAY OF PLAY?

❶ When you hear the word "play," how do you feel?

① You feel that play is an important part of life.

② You feel comfortable with the idea of play, but only in very small doses under extremely controlled circumstances.

③ You feel that play is for children. The idea of playing as an adult makes you feel very uncomfortable.

❷ What is your biggest concern about using your imagination?

① You don't have any concerns about it. You love to imagine new ideas.

② You are concerned that you might think of something that is embarrassing or shameful.

③ You're afraid of where your imagination might lead you.

❸ What is your biggest barrier to playing and imagining more?

① You wish you had more time to imagine and play.

② You're afraid of acting out some of your thoughts and fantasies.

③ You fear that if you start spending more time imagining and fantasizing that you will lose touch with reality.

Add up the scores (1, 2, or 3) on these three questions, and look below to consider what's in the way of play for you.

What's in the Way of Play?—Add It Up!

Total Score 3–4: Nothing. Play on, Macduff!

Total Score 5–6: You generally feel that imagination and play are the domain of children. Play and imagination can feel like an indulgence. We are going to talk about why this may be and hopefully make some changes so that you feel comfortable playing more often.

Total Score 7–9: You haven't allowed yourself to play in a long time, and you are afraid of what you might discover if you start to play. Let's explore this together so we can get you to use your imagination to dream up your next big thing.

If you found that you have difficulty playing these days, you are not alone. Imagination and play often get left by the side of the road in our adult lives, not because we experience a sudden shift in values at some turning point, but because we become distracted by the demands of daily life. As adults we take on responsibilities and do what we must do to survive. We relegate play and imagination to the status of a spare-time activity—what people often call a "hobby"—rather than making them central to our way of life. Many employers view imagination and creative play as extraneous or irrelevant indulgences. In fact, in some fields that are traditionally considered creative, imitation is far more valued than genuine inspiration.

However, to be fair, this is changing. Companies have recently begun to appreciate the value of play and imagination because they affect the quality of life of employees, drive innovation, and ultimately (though usually not immediately) contribute to the bottom line.

While play and imagination may not be critical for surviving, they are crucial for living a meaningful and joyful life. If you can't imagine what's next, how can you possibly get there?

PLAY AS A WAY OF CONNECTING »

When we stop playing and imagining we lose a sense of who we are and what is important to us. Yet that's just the tip of the proverbial iceberg. Without playing with ideas, we are not connecting with ourselves or other people. This leads to running in place and locking up when we try to dream up our next big thing.

Using your innate spirit of play to share your experiences and understanding with the world provides a way of borrowing from, and sharing with, those around you. It is also the most enjoyable way of connecting with other people. Play is essential, but it can also be challenging. Imagination and play may involve working through difficult or even unpleasant ideas. By its very nature play is unfinished—that is to say it doesn't have a defined beginning or ending or clear rules—so it can feel scary. Finding people with whom you can play is a vital part of life. I think of play as a barometer for emotional health. If you are playing—even a little bit, every day, things are probably going pretty well. If not, it's probably a good bet that you are running in place in some important ways. When you have a spirit of play in your job, relationships, and in yourself, these certain areas of your life will be flexible and strong; without it they will become rigid and brittle. And brittle things shatter.

Take some time to think about how play and imagination fit into your life right now. If you are having a hard time seeing how this may be relevant to you, consider how play, or the lack thereof, impacted my patient Tara's marriage.

Tara

Tara came to me in crisis.

A thirty-seven-year-old mother of two, Tara had been very successful in international finance. She worked her way up the ladder and was now working as a part-time consultant in order to take care of her family. Her husband, Ed, was a partner at his law firm.

As we began our work together Tara told me how she and Ed had met, about their courtship, and things they had shared. They were a great couple. They "worked." They had great jobs and bought a home together. Tara gave birth to a son, then a daughter two years later. Pressures mounted. They became stuck in their relationship roles and grew distant, fighting about everything and nothing. Then they stopped fighting because they stopped trying. That's when it really got bad.

They didn't feel safe to play with each other anymore. Tara was always expecting to be judged or scolded. Ed was just waiting to be nagged. Tara became uncomfortable sharing herself with Ed, so she stopped doing it. Ed withdrew as well. They retreated to their separate worlds. Loneliness and distance became the norm. They both directed their energy elsewhere: Tara focused on her son and Ed on his work.

On the day before Easter, Ed left his credit card bill in the bathroom trash. Tara noticed something odd so she picked it up. As she looked at it more carefully she saw a charge for a roundtrip flight from LAX to LAS about a month earlier. She knew he had been in Los Angeles on business, but he had never mentioned Las Vegas. Why was he there for barely twenty-four hours? Why would he bother returning to LA just to fly back home?

He was showering when she bolted into the bedroom to look at his phone.

That's when Tara saw the texts.

Things unraveled instantly.

When Tara learned about Ed's affair with Diana, Ed's colleague who had also become a close friend of hers, she felt punched and pummeled as more details came to light. This was her husband of nearly thirteen years. They had two kids together. A home. She knew him. She knew his habits, his desires, his secrets—yet each new revelation made her feel as though she were learning about a stranger.

She didn't know what she wanted to do next. It was too early. They agreed to go to couples counseling and each meet with their own individual therapist for now and take it from there.

When I asked her how she and Ed played together, she froze. "What do you mean, play?" she asked.

They didn't play. They worked. They planned. But they didn't play. Not anymore, anyway. Playing is fundamentally different from planning. Tara and Ed planned. A lot. But what they didn't do was play. They stopped imagining together, sharing their dreams with each other. Then life got complicated and reality got in the way. They grew apart and stopped trusting each other. It didn't take long for the quality of their relationship to ebb away. Ed's affair with Diana just made it official.

- -

» All Work and No Play

When people stop playing, exploring, and imagining, an important part of them dies. In couples, this effect can be intensified and disastrous because being a part of a union is about both working and playing; it involves imagining the future as well as being present in the here and now. Without working and playing you are not fully present. Both people may be working toward a future but if they are not playing and imagining their future together, they are two separate people who may share the same physical space but not the same emotional and psychological space. If you can't play and imagine together, you can't dream up a rich future together. You may be focused on tomorrow, but without new ideas and energy that vision can quickly become outdated—a stale business plan rather than an active shared dream. The future becomes about some vague idea of what you "should" do rather than a vision that you have crafted collectively. Couples that are not working *and* playing together are *not* united in the here and now together. This process can happen for individuals, couples, and families. I tend to work with individuals these days, and play is one of the first and most critical things I try to assess. One of the remedies for running in place is play and imagination.

» Playing as Adults

Fortunately, you already know how to play and imagine, even if it's been a while. It's just a matter of remembering how. You can think of your imagination as a muscle that hasn't been used in a while. You can rebuild. It just takes a little effort.

If it's been a while, we might just need to exercise it a bit.

For those of us who were not given full license to play as kids, developing our playfulness as adults can be a bit of a challenge. Adults play in many of the same ways that kids do: by using our minds' eyes to see ourselves in new and different ways, by considering who we are, and imagining who and what we can be.

Even if you played with abandon in your early years, it is possible to lose the spirit of play in adolescence as you labor under the demands of looking cool in front of peers or appearing capable or polished to parents. If you were fortunate enough to retain your spirit of play through your teens, it can still be siphoned out of your life when you enter adulthood due to the never-ending demands of making a living. Because many of us spend so little time imagining and playing, we may not know how to use our imaginations in a way that feels safe. I have heard many patients suggest that they have a hard time playing with ideas or different roles because they are afraid that they might encounter embarrassing or shameful thoughts.

One patient of mine, Ron, a professionally accomplished father of three, initially resisted the suggestion to try to explore his imagination when we began considering his next move. When I tried to get him to use play and imagination he said he didn't want to open "Pandora's Box" for fear that he would start to follow his impulses and "mess up" all of his personal stability and career success.

This fear—that delving into your imagination will lead you down the road to perdition is, unfortunately, all too common, but unfounded. If done properly, exploring your innermost ideas and fantasies will lead you toward redemption, not ruin. The fear is a barrier created by your inner critic, someone you'll get to know in Step Four. The threshold between reality and imagination is one that you must cross on your journey to Next—and the way across is with freedom and boundaries.

FREEDOM AND BOUNDARIES »

Exploring your sense of play helps you open your mind to new visions. Any random idea that you have may be helpful, even if it is not clear exactly how or where it fits. We want to open you up to the impossible without anything getting in the way of your imagination.

Your thoughts and feelings are a part of you—even the ones that you don't like. If you feel ashamed of something that comes to mind because it seems to reflect poorly on your moral character, remember: These are just thoughts. Regardless of whether you value your thoughts or ideas, or whether they bring you pride or shame, they are in your head, not outside of it. Acting on some of your thoughts may cause you and others great pain, but experiencing them in your mind cannot. Your mind wants to play with ideas, and it is far healthier (and effective) to explore them than to try to hold them back.

My professional experience has shown me that most of the time it is the repression of unwanted thoughts that causes problems, not the thoughts themselves.

If this feels foreign or uncomfortable to you, perhaps this little secret will bring you some relief: Everyone you know has thoughts and feelings that make them feel ashamed at times. You are no different—you are not "flawed" or "bad" because these images enter your consciousness. You are human. Nothing more. Nothing less.

Trying to wrestle unwanted thoughts to the ground and make them conform to your ideals leaves you depleted, confined, and ultimately stuck. Also, it doesn't work. Ironically trying to dominate your unwelcome ideas or feelings may provide more fuel for acting on them. Giving yourself permission to think your thoughts and experience your feelings is liberating and healthy as long as it is done properly.

Your thoughts don't always mean what you may think they mean. Try to suspend the urge toward certainty. Just because you once had a murderous thought about someone does not mean that you will, or even really want to, kill that person. It may just be your mind running through various wishes, fears, or possible courses of action. Almost everyone has thoughts that they don't like from time to time. One important note here: If you continue to ruminate about doing someone (or yourself) harm or you have a history of impulsive behavior or substance abuse, you should consult with a professional.*

*Although everyone has stray thoughts that they do not like and some of them may be just your imagination trying to work through a difficult problem or situation, it may be difficult to assess your own thoughts. If you feel that you, or anyone might be in danger, or you are not sure, seeking out a mental health professional is the best, and safest, course of action.

» Mr. Rogers' Neighborhood

One of the best models I have ever seen for how to use your imagination in a way that feels safe was Mr. Rogers. On the long-running public television show *Mr. Rogers' Neighborhood*, Fred Rogers always started and ended his show by singing the same songs, taking off his coat and shoes when he entered his house, and replacing them when he left. In the middle of the program the trolley ran through Mr. Rogers's house and entered the "Land of Make-Believe," where unexpected, fun, and wonderful things happened. Then the trolley came back and Mr. Rogers was there to sing a calm and bittersweet goodbye.

One of the reasons Fred Rogers's show inspired so many people (myself included) is that he embodied the ideal approach to imaginative play. He always greeted you in the exact same way before his trolley left. Once you were in the "Neighborhood of Make-Believe," everything was okay, including the unknown and unexpected, because you didn't worry that the play would go on too long or get out of control. Because of the framework he established, you had absolute faith that when the trolley returned to his house Mr. Rogers would be there, as calm, kind, and consistent as ever, to sing the goodbye song. This structure allowed you to let go of your fears, suspend your disbelief, and go with the trolley.

As we explore your future we will use a similar approach. We will aim for the ideal combination of freedom and boundaries, which will allow you to envision new possibilities without fear of where your mind might take you.

Imagining what's beyond the horizon requires the liberty of thinking and feeling without judgment and having appropriate boundaries so that you are *not* afraid you will take action on every thought, only the ones that you select. We will see that just because you can imagine new possibilities does not mean that you should, can, or will act on them. If you can embrace this concept you are well on your way to playing with ideas and taking one step closer to Next.

Remember: Our goal is to expand your possibilities, so once you are off playing and exploring, do not limit your imaginings. As intense as your thoughts and feelings can be, they are yours and yours alone. Try to suspend your judgment. All of your ideas and emotions are okay—scratch that. They are better than okay. They are essential for getting you where you need to go.

FROM PLAYING TO NEXT »

If you are feeling stuck, there is only one way out: in. We are going to use your imagination to bring you from the Now You to the New You. You need to play with ideas to envision what's next. I can help you get there, but make no mistake—you are the expert. The answers are inside of you. We just need the patience, confidence, and courage to bring them out. How do you get into the place where you can play without judgment but still retain the boundaries you need to keep you safe?

Let's start with location.

» Your Play Space

One of the greatest ideas from childhood that almost never comes with us when we get older is play space. Some of you were lucky enough to grow up with a space that was not your bedroom but a separate place that was dedicated to play—it might have been a recreation room or playroom, a tree house, or even a backyard. Remember that? Designating a room, or even part of a room, as an area for creative exploration is one of the best things you can do for a child or for an adult for that matter because it gives them permission to use their imaginations within the structure of a space that is set aside expressly for that purpose. Having the authority to open your mind in a designated area gives you both the freedom to imagine and the boundaries of knowing that whatever you dream up or create does not need to be subjected to the rules of reason or propriety that govern the rest of the world.

The idea of a play space may seem like an impossible luxury for kids, and an excessive indulgence for adults, but it is not—believe me, I've been living in New York City for almost twenty years, and I know a few things about space constraints. You just need to get creative to make yours. Your play space may not even necessarily be a physical location. It is about establishing a mental space or time where and when you are open to considering new ideas without judgment or recrimination. You can do this in your mind, but I have found that having a specific location or time becomes a marker, a signal that you can open the floodgates of your imagination to ideas you have never considered before.

As you start to think about your next step, consider putting aside some time in your day just to think and imagine possibilities for yourself. Wherever you think you can let your imagination run wild is where you should consider constructing your play space. You can do this in your car, on your train ride to work, or while you are making dinner. Personally, I play with new ideas at the very beginning of my work day. I try to get into my office as early as possible, when the city that never sleeps is still hitting the snooze button. I sit at my desk or in one of my office chairs and imagine new ways of being and jot down possibilities for future exploration or action. The only thing that matters is what works for you. Your location is less important than your orientation. The key is giving yourself the freedom to come up with new ideas or things that you want to do or be. At the beginning, it may be useful to pick a consistent time that has a defined beginning and end so you know when you will be open to exploration and when you have to put your imagining aside and deal with the pesky nuisance of reality.

For our next exercise, I want you to think about your ideal play space. This will be the space where you imagine what's next for you.

Exercise:

WHERE WILL YOU IMAGINE?

Write down on a piece of paper or in your journal a list of no more than ten words that describe your ideal play space.

For now, don't worry about whether this ideal is possible. Only consider what you want. Think about what might work best to help you open your mind. Should your play space be quiet or loud? Isolated or in public? Warm? Cold? What distractions might get in the way of letting your mind go? Do you have an attic? A basement? Perhaps a spare room in your house or office building? Is there a room at a local library that you could use to imagine your future?

Exercise:

WHEN WILL YOU IMAGINE?

Now that you have some ideas about *where* your ideal play space is, I want you to consider *when* you will be able to use this space. After all, having a place to play with ideas is not very helpful if you don't use it. I want you to think about when you will imagine what's next for you.

Write down on a piece of paper or in your journal your thoughts about the ideal time for you to imagine what's next.

Again, for now, don't worry about whether you have the time. We will come to that in Chapter 6 when we get you started on taking action. Just think about the best times during the day, week, or month that are usually best for you to let go and take time to imagine what's next for you. Are you a morning person? Would it be better to do it on your lunch break or after your kids have gone to sleep? Is this something that might need to change from day to day or week to week? Remember: the consistency of what time you choose to imagine is not nearly as important as your commitment to do it.

If your first ideas for a play space or play time don't pan out, keep trying new ones until something sticks. If it takes a while to find your space and time, you will appreciate it all the more. Play spaces can, and should, change over time, so if you have a spot that works for you and it suddenly stops feeling right, don't panic. The well is not dry, you might just need to find a new space.

» Your Play Tools

One of the other ways that people often get stuck in adulthood is through the use of language. Many of us spend so much time talking or writing that words, which certainly can be used to help get us moving with purpose, can end up getting in the way. This is exactly what happened to a patient of mine named Theresa, who was making a lot of money but felt very stuck in her job.

Theresa wore expensive scarves and tailored suits. She was never early or late for our sessions but always right on time. If I wore a watch, I would've been comfortable setting it by her. I have a pretty good memory, and I can't remember her ever arriving more than thirty seconds before or after our appointed time. And she never missed a session.

Theresa was doing great. She had a great job at a great company and made a great salary. She was smart and effective, and each year she stayed at her company she was given more responsibility and money and better and better titles. She liked feeling so competent and recognized. There was only one small problem:

She hated it.

Theresa told me she felt "suffocated" by her job. She was good at it but her success felt hollow because she was not expressing herself though her work. She had been very creative in high school. She acted in several plays and was a layout editor on her yearbook staff, but she stopped creating when she entered college. Now, three years after completing her graduate degree, she was well compensated and respected but felt stuck and unfulfilled. When I asked Theresa what she wanted to do that would allow her to use her creativity more, she said that she had no idea. She said that she needed to use a part of herself and share it with others, but she did not know what it was.

I encouraged her to make a list of her Activities of Joy (just like you did in Chapter 2) so that we could get a sense of who she was and what she might want to do next. Theresa agreed that this made sense—yet she didn't do it. Each week she would come to her session and say that she meant to write down her activities, but she was too busy to get to it. Theresa told me that she knew therapy was supposed to take work but that it was starting to feel like a job. As soon as she said "job," it hit me. The problem wasn't that she didn't want to make the list of her activities—the process itself was getting in the way.

That was when I decided to break out the crayons.

I suggested that Theresa use crayons to draw out her ideas in order to help us discover her natural language. She said she wasn't interested, but I could tell that she sort of was. So I started doing it myself. I grabbed a box of crayons and started drawing whatever came to mind. She did the same. It didn't yield much at first, but eventually she started drawing outside of sessions. She initially drew pictures of paintings that were in a gallery. She had never before consciously thought about painting or drawing in her life. So she considered it—for a while. She played with the idea of trying to paint and even bought a canvas and paints. It didn't take, but that didn't matter because the process of drawing got her mind moving again. Theresa eventually returned to her natural strength, which was her verbal skills, and tried creative writing for a while. She eventually used her skills to break into creative media and hasn't looked back.

It was the crayons that opened her up.

TOO MANY WORDS »

For Theresa, language and structure were the problem. She spent almost all of her days using her words, making lists, and constructing spreadsheets at her job, which she hated. So much of her time at work was spent with words and organization that she was burned out on them. Trying to use these methods to help her get unstuck was just digging her ditch wider and deeper.

Using crayons is not critical, just potentially helpful as you try to think about what's next for you. For example, even though Theresa's next step didn't ultimately require crayons, paints, or really any visual play tools, using the crayons helped get her mind moving again so she could draw a new horizon.

Does anything in Theresa's story sound familiar to you? Do you ever feel like words, lists, and plans are blocking you and getting in your way? If so, you may want to consider imagining what's next for you by using play tools.

When we are young we use lots of different tools to express ourselves. Paint, puppets, collage, blocks, colored pencils, and clay are all play tools that can be used to stimulate your imagination. One of the great things about crayons, pictures, or other nonverbal means of expression is that just by using them you may be able to access ways of thinking and feeling from long ago, before words got in your way. When we are very young and haven't yet learned to negotiate our world with words, which usually happens around age two, we think in feelings and images rather than in sentences and logic. Using play tools from childhood (e.g., crayons, markers, Play-Doh) can help you access some of your earliest thoughts and feelings, which can lead you to your natural language or help you decide what you want to express or do next.

It has been said that artists have somehow been able to preserve the essence of childhood thinking, and those who excel in creative fields are more successful at transforming these images and feelings into creations for others to experience. We *all* have these more primal thoughts, and they are still swirling around in our brains. It is just a matter of how we access them. I suggest doing it by actually breaking out play tools from your past. How do you do that? Keep reading.

Exercise:

WHAT ARE YOUR PLAY TOOLS?

Take a moment now and think back to your childhood. Were there certain play tools that you tended to use? What were they? Was there any activity that you could do for hours on end and not even notice that a moment had passed? Look back to some of your answers to the exercise from the last chapter about Activities of Joy from your past. Did you use any paint, puppets, modeling clay, Play-Doh, collage, or anything else when you were younger? Could you use them now in order to jump-start your imagination about what's next for you?

Now go out and get your play tools and play, play, play with abandon. I suggest you try using your play tools early and often; for this week, spend at least twenty minutes just playing. If it works, try doing it more. The more you open your mind to playing with new thoughts and ideas, the more comfortable you will become doing it. Your imagination is a muscle—use it or lose it.

When you imagine, don't worry about accomplishing or achieving anything in particular—just open your mind and let it run free. Leave the rules at the door. Whether you like to paint, make puppets, do collage, or mold with clay, go into your play space and just play. You'll be glad you did.

Once you're done, wash your hands and come on back. We need just a couple more pieces of the puzzle before we begin taking action on your next big thing. In the next step, we are going to pull together the pieces of you that we have gathered along the way in order to discover and define your personal purpose.

All aboard!

THE TAKEAWAY

1 You learned that play and imagination are critical parts of who you are. They helped you find the road ahead as a child and will help you navigate what's next for you as an adult.

2 You considered how much you currently play and imagine and what might be getting in the way of exploring your imagination.

3 You saw how play connects you to other people, especially those close to you.

4 You learned that freedom and boundaries are the keys to using your imagination in ways that feel both liberating and safe.

5 You explored the possibility of having a play space to help give you freedom and boundaries as you imagine what's next for you.

6 You considered using play tools from childhood, such as crayons, paints, or Play-Doh to help you get unstuck and consider your next step.

DISCOVER
YOUR
PURPOSE

Chapter

4

To move forward in life, you must make a choice about how you are living: If you can believe in or imagine a reason for your life and let your understanding guide you, then you are living a life of purpose. If you do not, or *can* not, you are not. Rediscovering your innate sense of play and cracking open your imagination will help you envision what's next for you, and as you will see in the chapters that follow, it is your actions that will get you there. But without purpose you cannot pass through to your next big thing. Purpose is your guide—your North Star that will lead you, follow you, and carry you when the days are dark and all seems lost.

Once you know your purpose, what's next usually just comes down to planning and execution, which will be the focus of Step Five, "Take Action," Step Six, "Embrace Your Process," and Step Seven: "Defeat the Three-Headed Monster: Passivity, Procrastination, and Perfectionism." For now, however, we need to focus on your purpose.

There is no right way to approach the idea of purpose. The only essential feature of purpose is that it is about *more* than you. When you are living a life of purpose your actions are directed toward something larger than yourself. Your purpose may involve your family, your faith, your spouse, a principle, an idea, or a belief—but what matters is that your actions are directed outside of just you.

People who are grounded in faith often instinctively gravitate toward the concept of purpose. Believing in God and living a life based on religious principles is a choice to orient your life to higher ideals. If religion is central to your purpose, you may consider using this step and the techniques throughout this book to explore your faith or to express and deepen your relationship to God.

If you're grounded in principles of science or philosophy, you can use the quizzes, exercises, and techniques in this chapter and beyond to elaborate further on your ideas or the beauty you see around you in order to create meaning for you and those around you.

A GUIDE TO YOUR ACTIONS »

If you are not inclined toward religion, philosophy, or science, but still want help deciding and acting on your next big thing, use the suggestions in this book, and especially in this chapter, to help establish a trajectory to guide you and push you further along your path.

If you have spent some time considering your life path, the idea of personal purpose may strike a chord for you, and the exercises in this chapter may help you just tighten your current understanding. If this is an unfamiliar or uncomfortable concept, you may want to use this chapter to develop a temporary purpose, because having something to drive you is a key to getting you moving forward. Even if the idea of purpose rubs you the wrong way, at the very least, some of these ideas can help you enrich the lives of those around you and bring them closer to you.

The following two exercises will help prepare you to craft your Statement of Personal Purpose, the ultimate goal of this step and chapter. This first exercise is designed to get you to think big; the second one is aimed at getting you to think far. I suggest that you write down your answers to both exercises in your notebook—even a few words or ideas will do. You do not need to have complete answers, just enough to stretch your mind.

Exercise:

NO LIMITS

1. If you were wealthy beyond reason and no longer had to work for a living but instead could do whatever you wanted, what would you do?

2. If you were given the opportunity to create your own sixty-second spot during the Super Bowl, where you could say whatever you wanted to say or show whatever you wanted the world to see, what would you do? Would you make something entertaining, funny, sad, challenging, thought provoking?

3. If you found that you could make one lasting change in the world that would be guaranteed to affect people long after you are gone, what would you make?

4. If you could create an organization or company that could make or do something and you were guaranteed of its phenomenal success, what would that company do? How would it affect people's lives? Would it make life easier, healthier, or more enjoyable?

You may not know the answers to many or any of these questions, which is fine. You don't have to. The key for now is to let the questions stimulate your mind and orient you toward what is meaningful to you. Later in this chapter we will use these thoughts to craft your personal Statement of Purpose. Once you have your purpose, you can use it to make meaning and guide your path.

» What Is Your Personal Legacy?

Another approach to thinking about your purpose is considering your personal legacy.

Throughout the course of our lives, each of us has an opportunity to do or make something that serves as a representation of who we are. When we use our energy for good, we can leave something behind. It can be a symbol, a statement, a declaration that we were here, proof that we played our part. What we develop is the evidence that we made a tangible contribution. It's a physical manifestation of our spirit, an affirmation that we donated to the world, and a confirmation of our unique addition to history.

Although you may not know how you fit into the grand scheme, by simply creating something and sharing your creation with others, you have contributed. If you can suspend your skepticism and transcend disbelief long enough to embrace this process, you can create meaning through your actions. In doing so, you can take comfort in the knowledge that you have given back, perpetuated the cycle of energy, and donated to and replenished the world.

One exercise that I have used to help patients envision their purpose involves imagining the future and focusing on the life of a descendant many years from now. This next exercise is designed to get you to think far, far beyond now, to a time when you are no longer here.

Exercise:

YOUR GREAT-GREAT-GRANDDAUGHTER

Take a few moments now to imagine your great-great-granddaughter. If you don't have children, then picture your great-great-grandniece. If you don't have siblings, envision the great-great-granddaughter of a friend. If you don't have any friends, make one today and then picture his or her great-great-granddaughter. The point is, try to think of a specific person who will be here in the world long after you have passed. Imagine her clearly.

Put this book down for at least a minute or two to get a clear picture of your great-great-granddaughter in your mind. What's her name? Where does she live? What kind of world does she live in? Get to know her. How is she getting on in the world? Think about her relationships, who she talks to, and what she eats for breakfast.

Close your eyes and try to imagine her as vividly as you see this book in front of you. Spend some time thinking about her.

Now that you have gotten to know your great-great-granddaughter, turn the camera back on you. Try to imagine her thinking of you: What does she know about you? What does she do to thank you for how you contributed to her life? Why is she lucky and proud to be your great-great-granddaughter? What did you create that she can appreciate or that improves her experience of the world?

Ask yourself what you contributed to her and her world. What did you leave of yourself that enriched her life? How did you inspire her? Did you write a poem or build her a house or make her a quilt? Maybe it was the company you built that made colored sand. Did you build a house, a park, a landscape, or a beautiful garden? Did you create a self-swinging park swing or some other invention that made her life easier or more enjoyable? What about the book you wrote about the relative merits of snickerdoodle cookies when compared to lemon bars? Perhaps it was the soundtrack for the movie about the founding of Boise, Idaho, that you scored? Or was it the recording of the interpretative dance you developed? Was it the photos you took of birds or barns or urban decay? Maybe it was the research you published on why we yawn.

Try to suspend any judgments about what you left her. For now, only consider if you have given her something. Imagine something tangible that your great-great-granddaughter has, that she can experience in some way, that you made for her.

Spend some time considering this thought. What will your contribution be? If you need to take a few minutes, hours, or days to wrap your head around this, then by all means, do so.

If you are having a difficult time picturing how you might contribute to your great-great-granddaughter's life, don't fret. If you haven't spent much time imagining a person who does not yet exist, you are not alone. Remember Amanda, whom you met back in Chapter 1 when she was running in place? This is how the exercise went for her:

Amanda

I knew that Amanda had been working and supporting herself since the age of fourteen. She had been essentially living from paycheck to paycheck since that time and felt trapped by her financial situation. Understandably, she became focused only on survival. But over time, it left her feeling depleted and stuck. Her eyes had become trained to look down, but she needed to look up, toward the horizon.

I tried to get Amanda to "look up" by first removing the obstacle of money. I asked her to imagine for a moment that she didn't need to work for a living. If she were independently wealthy, what would she do with her time?

She said that she had no idea what she would do. Working was just what she did. She had a daughter to support. From time to time, she had fantasized about moving to Hawaii—but other than that, nothing came to mind. When she returned the next week, Amanda told me that other than a vague fantasy of moving to a warm place with a view of the ocean, she didn't know what she would do if she didn't have to work.

I asked Amanda to imagine her daughter Hannah as an old woman. She closed her eyes and tried to picture her nine-year-old daughter as a grandmother. I asked Amanda to try to picture how she might contribute to her great-great-granddaughter's life. Were there tangible things that she could do now that could be shared with her great-great-granddaughter?

Amanda was quiet. I could see the tension and searching behind her closed eyelids and in the tiny muscles around her eyes. She opened them gradually and said she could only think of one thing—that she might make some jewelry that her great-great-granddaughter could wear to her senior prom.

That was all she needed to get started.

After refining her vision further, Amanda was intrigued by the idea that she should pursue jewelry making. Creating with her hands and knowing that other people were enjoying her jewelry helped define her. Through making jewelry she could play, work, and contribute to others' happiness. In addition, she would leave something of herself to others, including her great-great-granddaughter. This gave her focus and purpose.

Even if you don't plan to create jewelry for your great-great-granddaughter to wear to her senior prom, there are countless other ways to leave some part of yourself to her. How will you leave your mark? How will you create your sense of purpose?

Before we craft your personal Statement of Purpose, which will guide you throughout the rest of the book, I have one more exercise for you. I have used this exercise from time to time with patients who have a hard time accessing their purpose through imagining their lives without limits or considering the legacy they would leave behind.

Exercise:

NOTHING LEFT TO LOSE

Imagine for a moment that you found out that in one year's time you will vanish from Earth. Pretend that you know this as a certainty. Three hundred and sixty-five days from right now, you will no longer be here. Write down a list of no more than twenty things that you will do during this year. What is most important to you? Do you want to go somewhere? See something?

Meet someone? Do or make something? Take your time—but not too much time, and think about the things that you would want to do this year.

Okay, you are primed. You have opened up your mind and your imagination. You know what brings you joy and what you value. You know what you would do if you had no limits. You know what kind of legacy you might want to leave, and you know what you would do if you had a definite time limit on your life. The time has come to pull it all together, to define your personal purpose.

YOUR PERSONAL PURPOSE »

If you ever applied to college or for an internship, or filled out forms at a career-counseling center, you have undoubtedly written a "Statement of Purpose." I hate those things. Most "Statements of Purpose" are worthless because they have nothing to do with your *real* purpose; they are written for the admissions committee or human resources department personnel who will make a decision whether to grant you admission or give you a job. When you write a statement like that for an audience, you do the smart thing and write the answers that you think they will want to read. Therefore, the statements of purpose you have written in the past have only been useful to you in the sense that they let the admissions counselors or human resources people assess if you know anything about how to market yourself. Marketing yourself is an important skill, to be sure, but not one that is related to your real purpose as a human being.

The Statement of Purpose that you will create now will be nothing like that.

I don't really care whether you are good at marketing yourself, only whether I can help you articulate your personal purpose. In fact, feel free not to show your Statement of Purpose to anyone. Of course, you are welcome to do so, but in truth, there is no need. This is fundamentally between you and yourself. That's it. No one else needs to know about it. If you think that showing your statement to other people (or thinking that you might show it to other people) could impact what you write and get in the way of your being honest with yourself, I would suggest that you keep it to yourself. For now, I want you to use the thought experiments from this chapter to help inform your thinking about what is important to you—what gives you purpose.

If you already know your purpose and what gives you meaning, you may be wondering why you are bothering to write this out. Actually taking the time to write a true Statement of Purpose helps you in several important ways. It helps you to:

- **Improve your self-awareness.** Writing down what is important to you draws your attention to yourself and lays out a template for your personal path.
- **Respect and appreciate who you are.** By setting aside the time to write down your purpose you are implicitly valuing yourself and your ideas. Producing this document reminds you of your possibilities and contributes to your self-esteem. Experiences in your past that once seemed pointless or harmful are given meaning because they have contributed, either directly or indirectly, to your Statement of Purpose.
- **Define and live your priorities.** Through the act of writing your Statement of Purpose, you make choices about what to express and how to express it. In actually putting these ideas to paper you are choosing what to include and what to omit. This helps you define what you value and what is nonessential, which can improve your ability to make choices about how you spend your time.
- **Develop yourself.** Through stretching your imagination and thinking about your choices, you will consider yourself in new ways, which helps you grow intellectually and emotionally.
- **Improve your relationships.** As you develop a greater understanding of who you are through the act of writing your personal purpose, it becomes easier to make good choices about the people in your life. Seeing yourself in a new light helps you place a higher value on yourself and your possibilities. This allows you to appreciate those who

contribute to your life and path. You will also be less likely to spend time with those who don't treat you properly and help you on your journey. The comfort level you have with yourself will make you more at ease with others, which will contribute to stronger relationships.

- **Deepen your capacity for generosity.** When you know yourself better and are more at ease with the person you are, you will find greater comfort in giving of yourself to others. In fact, sharing yourself is an essential part of getting to your next big thing. It will be the final step of our journey together. As you craft your Statement of Purpose you will establish who you are and what you need. This will help you recognize and identify with these qualities in others. Your increased self-assurance, self-awareness, and empathy for other people will lead you to want to share with those around you.

Convinced? Great. Let's get down to it. If not, why not do it anyway? What do you have to lose?

Exercise:

YOUR STATEMENT OF PURPOSE

Look over all of the work you have already done. Consider where you are running in place and what you want to change. Review your roles, Activities of Joy, and especially your values from Chapter 2. If you wrote down a list of aspirational roles back in Chapter 2, take time out now and consider how they can be a part of your life going forward. Open up your mind and imagination as you did in Chapter 3 and skim the exercises you did in this chapter, all of which were meant to get you thinking bigger and farther. Let it all wash over you.

Now take out a sheet of paper or journal and attack this exercise with passion and fury. This is all about you—and about transforming the Now You to the New You.

Your personal Statement of Purpose should include the following information:

1. **Your name.**
2. **Between one and three things that are important to you. Begin with the words, "I believe in . . ."** *(Please do not put down more than three. This is not a term paper but a document aimed at focusing you on what gives you meaning.)*
3. **Two or three sentences with concrete actions you'd like to take in the future that allow you to express and live these things in your daily life. Begin the sentences with the words, "I will use my time to . . ." or "I will use my talents to . . ." or "The action I will take is . . ."**

Now for the kicker: Your Statement of Purpose should be no more than 100 words. That may seem hard to do, but imposing limits forces you to be direct and to the point. We will deal with details later. For now, just do it.

You may want to consider why these things are important to you, but don't put that down here. Your statement should be brief. It should be a broad declaration of your priorities and a general idea about what you want to do to promote and live your values. The statement should be based in the present but aimed at the future.

Here are a few examples of what your statement of purpose might look like:

- *My name is Jane Doe.* I believe in the power of education to improve the future. I believe teaching children how to be compassionate human beings is the foundation for cooperation and charity. I will develop and deploy my skills as a kindergarten teacher to teach children and ultimately teach other teachers how to teach compassion and charity for other students.
- *My name is John Doe.* I believe in the power of technology to make life easier for people with disabilities. I believe in the need for improving the quality of life for people suffering from Alzheimer's disease and other

age-related illnesses. I will develop and deploy my skills in technology to help improve people's memory and assist those living with this disease.

- *My name is Jen Doe.* I believe in family, education, and faith. I will be a strong mother for my children and wife for my husband. I will set an example for my family about the values that I believe in. I will do everything I can to help my children succeed in school and do all I can to make sure that they graduate from college. I will go to church every week and encourage my husband and children to do the same.

- *My name is Jan Doe.* I believe in entrepreneurship to raise the standard of living for all people by increasing innovation and economic wealth. I will come up with a kitchen device that allows people to speak to their stoves and refrigerators that will make cooking and multitasking in the kitchen easier. I will use my talents as an entrepreneur to develop a prototype and create a brand new company to market my device that will allow me to enjoy financial success and bestow this success upon others.

- *My name is Jim Doe.* I believe in the power of government to improve people's lives. I believe in promoting industry, investing in the future of energy, improving health for all citizens, and protecting the rights of children and the environment. I will use my talents as a politician to work for these causes and improve the lives of citizens in my country and ultimately around the world.

- *My name is Jonathan Doe.* I believe in God and the need to live by His dictates as set forth in the Bible. I believe in promoting His word and teachings to all who are ready to receive them. I will spend my time learning more about His teachings and developing my talents as a public speaker in order to share His message.

- *My name is Janelle Doe.* I believe in the power of comedy to connect with others and communicate sophisticated ideas that can help people live happier and more meaningful lives. I believe in equal rights for all people regardless of gender, race, age, class, disability, and sexual orientation. I am especially interested in equal rights within the entertainment industry. I will use my talents as a comedian to entertain people and shed light on these issues and inform the national and international conversation.

Everything that we have done up until now has been aimed at getting you to this point. Getting to know yourself in Step One, imagining yourself in Step Two, and the exercises in Step Three have all been about getting you to imagine your purpose. Now it's time to put the pen to paper (or the fingers to touchscreen—you get the gist). This may be a challenge for you, but it is important and will inform the next steps on our journey together.

You can do it.

Take your time. Make it count.

I'll see you when you get back.

. . .

If you were able to write out your Statement of Purpose, or even part of your statement, congratulate yourself. This is a victory. Even if it doesn't feel like it, it is. Your purpose is what will bring you to the next big thing in your life. Your statement doesn't need to be perfect; it just needs to be done. You are moving on. You have purpose.

In the next section we are going to move away from imagination, play, and purpose. We will come back to them later.

If this was particularly difficult for you or you were not able to get much traction on your Statement of Purpose, do not fear: There is a good reason why you are having difficulty: It is your inner critic. It's time to deal with him. In our next step you will learn to recognize, face, and pass through your inner critic. If you didn't craft your personal Statement of Purpose just yet, you can come back to it after you have learned to face him. In fact, even if you found it easy to write your Statement of Purpose, you will want to know how to deal with your critic, because if he hasn't shown up yet, he will.

The only way past him is through him. Let's meet your inner critic face to face.

THE
TAKEAWAY

1 You learned that purpose is the third part of your personal foundation. You need play and imagination to help you envision your next steps, and you need work to get you there, but purpose is what guides your actions.

2 If you can imagine a reason for your life and use that vision to guide your actions, then by definition, you are living a life of purpose.

3 You learned that purpose helps inform your understanding of your life, because when you know your purpose you can make sense of your past in order to shape your future.

4 You began to consider your purpose by envisioning a life with no limitations, thinking about your personal legacy, imagining how you will have contributed to your great-great-granddaughter, and contemplating what you would do if you had nothing left to lose.

5 You wrote out your true Statement of Purpose and celebrated this as a personal victory.

PART

II

Facing Your Demons

FACE
YOUR INNER
CRITIC

Chapter

5

There comes a time in all our lives when we hit a wall and want to retreat. That time may come sooner or it may come later, but it *will* come. Just as there is a hero inside of you (whom you will learn to embrace in Chapter 9) who wants you to dream and move boldly toward a bright and exciting horizon, there is also a part of you that wants to slow you down and stop you in your tracks. That part of you, that voice, will whisper in your ear, menace you, and if you *still* don't listen to him, then he'll get nasty. If he hasn't made an appearance yet, don't be fooled—he will.

As you begin to move from thinking to doing, this voice usually gets louder. It is the voice inside of you that is full of harsh judgment and criticism. The voice is an expert in sabotaging your best-laid plans to envision a better future and attack it with passion and fury. It is the voice that says, "Stop," "You can go no farther," and "Go back to how you were before."

It is the voice of your inner critic. There is no avoiding him.

You can't go around him.

You can't go above him.

And you certainly can't tunnel beneath him—he can get down pretty low.

The only way past him is through him.

Let's go there together.

FROM THINKING TO DOING »

In the next step on our journey you will move from thinking to doing. This is usually—though not always—where the inner critic makes his presence known. That is why this step is all about facing him and going through him. I will not promise that it will be easy, but it is critical. If you don't do it, your inner critic will take over your show. And it's not his show; it's yours. If you don't run it, he will, so let's put you back in charge. There are plenty of haters out there, and we will deal with them in time. For now, let's reduce the number of haters by one by starting with your inner critic.

As you get closer to what's next and begin taking actions based on your Statement of Purpose, your inner critic will be there to set up roadblocks to slow you down. He will raise your anxiety, inhibit your imagination, and torpedo your plans. If you focus on his criticism you will be less motivated to take your next step—I mean, why would you want to do anything if you just expect to be scolded, criticized, and cut down? Listening to your critic will cause you to feel more stressed and sad.

Everyone has an inner critic. It's just that not everyone knows how to identify him. Before we meet yours, let's take a moment to let you describe you to yourself so we know exactly what we are dealing with here. This exercise is going to be different from the exercise we did in Chapter 2, when you got to know yourself by looking at your roles; your roles because are on the outside. They are how the world sees you. In order to get a pulse on your inner critic, we need to start by getting to know how you see yourself on the inside.

Exercise:

THE INSIDE YOU

Write down a list of up to ten adjectives that you would use to describe you to yourself and *only to yourself*. This last part is absolutely essential in order for you to be totally (and possibly brutally) honest. Do not plan to share this information with anyone. There are no right or wrong answers, just the words in your mind.

If this is a bit unusual or confusing, there's a good reason why: You probably don't spend too much time describing you to yourself. To help you along, here are some examples of lists from four separate people with whom I worked in the past, each of whom came to me because they felt that they were running in place in vastly different ways:

1. **Patient 1:** Honest, anxious, careful, people pleaser, detail oriented, forthright, religious, fearful, wishful, loyal, devoted.

2. **Patient 2:** Optimistic, open, domineering, driven, self-righteous, family oriented, unattractive, thoughtful, romantic, opportunistic.

3. **Patient 3:** Handsome, bold, ladies' man, alcoholic, forgetful, charming, rich, strong, confident, shameless.

4. **Patient 4:** Smart, accomplished, bored, nervous, clumsy, clean up well, lucky, loyal, worried, put others before me.

Would you use any of these words to portray you to yourself? If not, find ones that do. Make a list of up to ten words that you feel best describe who you are, but again, keep it to ten or less—we don't want you going on all night. Take your time. I'll be here when you get back.

Welcome back. I hope you were able to generate a list of words that you feel reflects your current self-perception. Now that you've created it, let's break it up and break it down.

Exercise:

BREAK IT UP—BREAK IT DOWN

Look at the words you wrote down. In all likelihood, some of them are words that you would consider to be positive words, such as "honest," "loyal," "smart," "accomplished," etc. Other words are more negative, like "unattractive," "wounded," "worried," etc. Split your list into two: The list on the left should have positive words; the list on the right should have negative words. If there are some words on your list that you don't think of as particularly positive or negative, feel free to leave them off of these lists.

Here's how Patient 1's list broke down:

POSITIVE ADJECTIVES	NEGATIVE ADJECTIVES
Honest	Anxious
Detail oriented	People pleaser
Forthright	Fearful
Religious	
Loyal	
Devoted	

Study both of your lists carefully. Once you have really soaked in the positive and negative adjectives that you use to describe yourself, place your left hand over your list of positive adjectives and look again at your list of negative adjectives.

The list you are looking at does not come from you. It comes from your inner critic.

It's time to deal with him.

WHO IS YOUR INNER CRITIC? »

Your inner critic is the part of you that tells you, "You can't." He is powerful and clever. He has been with you since childhood. But he hasn't been with you forever—even if it feels that way sometimes.

When we are born, since we are weak and fragile, we must rely on older, stronger, and more experienced people to take care of us. As we grow and learn, the world around us can seem vastly different depending on our circumstances. In the best-case scenario we are fortunate enough to be raised in an environment of consistent love and appropriate boundaries. When this happens perfectly (it never does), our sense of helplessness is diminished and we feel safe and happy. We look at the world with joy and wonder and learn about our natural strengths and how we can influence the world around us. In the worst-case scenario we are given scant support, consistency, or safety. Perhaps we were abandoned, abused, or traumatized. The latter situations highlight our weakness and often lead us to experience the world as a frightening and unpredictable place that should be approached with fear, if it should be approached at all.

In all likelihood, your circumstances are somewhere between these two extremes. You (I hope) had moments when you felt safe and loved, though you probably also had times when you felt alone, out of control, and afraid. If you experienced the world as frightening and unpredictable—and everyone does at one point or another—you used the best asset you had to get through and push forward. When you felt scared, helpless, or dominated by the outside world, you did the best you could to get by. You used your imagination to create a world inside of yourself. Instead of accepting the world as unpredictable and arbitrary, which would have been overwhelming, you attempted to bring order to the chaos by trapping it inside your mind. You tried to manage your terror by creating a voice that gave you rules to follow so that you wouldn't feel helpless.

That voice is your inner critic.

When I talk about feeling "overwhelmed, helpless, or dominated," I don't mean to imply that you were necessarily traumatized as a child, though sadly, many people have been. As I mentioned before, we all feel out of control or powerless at one time or another in our lives, especially when we are very young. As a result, everyone has an inner critic. The tone and nature of your critic will depend on your particular circumstances. Even if you grew up in an ideal home environment, with well-meaning caregivers or parents who were trying to protect you or teach you how to behave, you would have felt helpless and overwhelmed sometimes.

THE SEEDS OF YOUR INNER CRITIC »

Let's go back to our example from Chapter 3, when we were talking about play and imagination as natural strategies for dealing with new and frightening situations. In our example, you were three years old and you suddenly found out that your parents would be having a new baby boy. You used play and imagination to get you through the uncertainty and fear of being displaced. Now let's go a little further into this scenario.

Imagine that your parents have just returned from the hospital with their new bundle of joy. It is an exciting and confusing time. You quickly realize that this is a bum deal. Your parents are suddenly focusing much of their efforts and attention on the little guy who, frankly, doesn't seem all that impressive to you. In fact, he seems pretty lame. Suddenly you have to share everything and everyone with him. Will there be enough? Will they take care of you? Why are they always smiling at him? You are . . . displeased, to say the least.

Two months go by. You, Mom, and baby brother are about to leave the house to go to the pediatrician for his checkup. Mom turns her back to get her keys. Little brother is sleeping in his car seat by the door. But this is your playtime. Why is this happening? Will they ever play with you again? You have had it. You express your frustration and bonk him on the head. He wakes up, startled and wailing. Your mother whips around to see what happened. She instantly realizes that you hit your little brother. She goes to comfort him, then turns to you and shoots you a look that could melt lava. She yells that you are a "bad child."

Your mother has reason to be angry. She has a job to protect your brother and you, of course, but calling you a "bad child" is too much. You are not "bad." True, what you did was not kind, but it does not make you a "bad child," just a frustrated one who was expressing herself in the only way she knew how. You know that what you did was wrong and you take that in, but you also trust your mother's judgment, so you ingest the "bad child" label as well. Remember now, you are three years old. You have to trust her judgment. If your mother calls you "bad," it hurts, but she must be right. She can't be wrong because you rely on her for food, protection, and love, and if her perception of the world is wrong, well, that is a much more frightening thought for you.

In fact, the idea that you are "bad" might actually be useful to you if it helps you to understand and gain control over your world. Subconsciously you consider this and wonder if your being "bad" is the reason why everyone has been smiling with delight at your little brother but not at you. It's all very mixed up. You try to soak it in and process it. You begin to wonder if you are a "bad" or "good" child.

You don't want to be a bad child, but even more frightening is the idea that being "good" or "bad" is outside of your control. You look for rules to help make sense of it all. In all the confusion, you try to find something that guides you. You imagine—you create—a voice that helps you navigate the chaos. The voice tells you how to act and, more importantly, how *not* to act so you don't feel that way again. After more experiences like this, the voice becomes distorted, consolidated, powerful. Layers form above it and it may gain or lose steam as you grow.

These are the seeds of your inner critic, who eventually takes on a life of his or her own. The development of your critic depends largely on your personality, experiences, and environment. If you grew up in a generally supportive home, your critic may be weak and easy to manage. If you had a tough parent who was rigid and harsh but predictable, your critic will likely be similar in nature to her or him. If you experienced trauma or abuse, your critic may be intense, powerful, and arbitrary. Experience has taught me that this is the most difficult type of critic to unseat, though when you do, the joy you will experience is far greater than words can describe.

Before you turn to face your inner critic, let's take a moment to size him up so we know who we are dealing with here.

Exercise:

SIZE HIM UP

Look back at the lists of positive and negative adjectives you created earlier in this chapter. Add up the number of negative adjectives you wrote down, and then add up the number of positive adjectives. Did you have more negative or positive adjectives, or were they the same?

If your lists were about even or you had more positive words than negative words, the struggle ahead may not be as bad as you think it will be. In contrast, if you had significantly more negative words than positive ones, expect a more drawn-out process.

Now look at each word on your list of negative adjectives and assign each word a number from 1 to 10, with 1 indicating that you feel this quality describes you only weakly or rarely and 10 indicating that it is a word that describes a significant and fundamental aspect of who you are.

Let's return to our example from earlier and look at Patient 1's negative adjectives. You will notice that she assigned high numbers to many of her negative adjectives, indicating that she sees herself as a highly anxious person.

Negative Adjectives

Anxious (8)

People pleaser (7)

Fearful (9)

Analyzing how strongly you feel these negative adjectives describe you is a good indicator of the strength of your inner critic. The higher the numbers, the stronger the inner critic you will be facing.

If you see that you wrote down far more negative words than positive words and you have a lot of high numbers next to your negative adjectives, you may feel daunted. That is understandable, but it's better to know what you are dealing with so you can get through your inner critic and take action on what's next for you.

SEPARATING FROM YOUR CRITIC »

It may seem a bit confusing to try to segregate a part of your inner emotional life. After all, your inner critic has been a fundamental part of you—a psychological squatter, if you will—but it is absolutely essential that you do. If you think that you are just a naturally negative person and your "inner critic" is you, you're wrong. You are actually a positive person, even if you don't know it or believe it yet (more on this in Chapter 9). The time has come to get some distance from your inner critic. You've already taken the first step, by beginning to recognize and understand him. Now we are going to take it up a notch: We are going to separate you from your inner critic.

I know that this might seem a bit kooky to you—I've heard it all before. But separating from your inner critic is not insane. It's courageous. It is a declaration that you are taking action on your next big thing. If this feels odd, that's good. It probably means that you are beginning to look at yourself in a whole new way. Don't let the newness startle you. Consider how this process went for my patient Amanda, whom you first met way back in Chapter 1 and encountered again in Chapter 4.

Amanda

Amanda had been doing so well. She was making progress and making jewelry, doing more, and feeling better about herself. She ended up in a conversation about her jewelry with a woman who ran a jewelry store in SoHo. Upon the woman's request, Amanda brought in some pieces for her to display and sell. A few days later, the woman called to tell her that the pieces were getting a lot of buzz and that a couple of them had already sold. That was when Amanda realized that things were actually changing.

Amanda saw a new image of herself that confused her. "Who does this?" she thought. Who is this woman who at the age of forty-one starts making jewelry—something she had always wanted to do but couldn't acknowledge—and finds a receptive public that is willing to pay her for it? It was as if one morning she woke up, got out of bed, looked in her bathroom mirror, and saw a stranger staring her in the face. She didn't know who she was or what to do.

Suddenly, Amanda was out there on the edge—on the verge of something new, and she was afraid. Amanda wanted change and now here it was, staring her in the eyes and she wanted to retreat. So she did what most people do: she bolted back to the familiar. She didn't collect her money from the store owner and stopped making jewelry. Amanda also went back to an ex-boyfriend who mistreated her, whom she had dumped earlier in our work together when she was feeling stronger. She sensed that she'd been derailed but couldn't put her finger on what exactly happened, or why. Amanda felt ashamed that she stopped moving forward, but she didn't want to make it worse by feeling embarrassed. She tried to ignore it. And she ignored me. Amanda stopped coming to therapy for a few weeks, something she had never done before.

When she returned to my office I welcomed her back and told her I thought that her inner critic was at the helm. I had never used the term "inner critic" in our sessions before, but the label immediately struck a chord for her.

Amanda understood what I meant by an inner critic, but her critic had been running her life for "as far back as forever," as Amanda put it. She found it hard to see her critic as just a part of her rather than all of her. She thought, "Well, this is who I am. I'm just a negative person, and there's nothing I can do about it." Her critic had become so fundamental to her identity that she found it hard to distinguish her critic's voice from her own.

"That's nonsense," she said. "There's no critic. That's just me."

That moment is deeply etched in my mind because my response to Amanda was so automatic and unexpected. I didn't even think. I barely processed what she said when I retorted, "The greatest trick the devil ever played was convincing the world he did not exist."*

She got it immediately.

It was time to separate them.

- -

Just like Amanda, you might think that there is no inner critic and that the negative voice in your mind is just you. But it's not. It's your inner critic, and he is only a part of you, not all of you. If he is strong enough it can be hard to hear his voice as distinct from the voice inside of you that wants to reach out and grab a brighter future.

For Amanda, the experience of seeing her inner critic as separate from her felt very strange at first, as it might to you, but it is crucial that you do. Ignoring your critic won't make him or her go away.

It will just make him stronger.

*This quote, which I must admit I picked up from the movie *The Usual Suspects*, has been attributed to the nineteenth-century French poet Charles Baudelaire.

HOW DO YOU DEFEAT YOUR INNER CRITIC? »

How do you defeat your Inner Critic? The answer to this question is simple: You don't.

Your inner critic is not malicious, just misdirected. He is not your enemy, but he *is* the enemy of your next big thing. Therefore, you need to respect your inner critic like a friend, but be wary of him like an enemy.

Remember: Your critic developed in order to help you cope with a sense of helplessness or to make sense of confusion or chaos you experienced when you were younger. He is not bad. In fact, he's good. Well, at least he is filled with good intentions. He's looking out for you and wants to protect you. That's the reason he has been useful to you for so long. Even if you could get rid of him entirely, you wouldn't want to. Think of your critic as a well-intended but misguided grandfather who loves you and wants to protect you at all costs. In the name of keeping you safe and helping you avoid embarrassment or shame your inner critic wants to keep you grounded—immobilized. Instead of telling you that he loves you dearly, more than anything in the world really, he expresses his deep fear that something will happen to you by telling you that you should never leave your house.

Your critic tries to keep you safe by making the world feel predictable and ordered. He gives you rules to follow, and when you break them you become fearful of what will happen next. What's next is, by definition, unknown. And your critic is afraid of the unknown. To your fearful critic, "unknown" is a synonym for "danger," which is exactly what he wants you to avoid. Your inner critic has been in power for too long and in the interest of keeping you safe, has also been keeping you from believing in your possibilities and trying new things. Think about how he has served you in the past, but remember, he's just not necessary for getting to what's beyond your horizon. You may need him again later, but for now you just need some space.

So now you know that you can't defeat your inner critic and you can't let him defeat you, which probably has you wondering what you should do. The answer to this question is the same as the answer to every impossible question: one step at a time.

First you are going to:

1. **Turn Up the Volume**—on your inner critic so that you can hear him clearly.

Then you will

2. **Face the Abyss**—of fear and doubt that he has been pushing.

Finally, you are going to

3. **Choose**—between fear and faith.

Are you ready?
We're going in.
Hold on to something.

TURN UP THE VOLUME »

In order to turn up the volume on your inner critic I want you to try to use your imagination, which, thanks to the exercises you did in Chapter 3, is now primed and ready to go. Think about your inner critic as a separate part of you. It may seem like an odd thing for a clinical psychologist to tell you to personify and even address a voice inside your head, but doing this can help you get some much-needed distance from your inner critic. The space that we are going to open up together will allow you to disentangle yourself from the pessimist in your house who has been holding on too tightly and causing you to run in place. We are going to exploit the distance between you and your critic so that you are much more likely to allow yourself to take action on what's next. Once you have made that separation you may not exactly be home free, but you are well on your way.

TURN UP THE VOLUME ON YOUR INNER CRITIC

Take out your notebook, etc., and jot down answers to the following questions. If you don't have answers to all of them, just answer the ones that pertain to your inner critic.

1. What does your inner critic sound like?
2. Does he have a male voice or a female voice?
3. Does he sound like you, like somebody you know, or like someone from your past?
4. Whose voices contributed to your critic?
5. How did he/she become distorted?
6. What experiences helped make her powerful?
7. Can you think of times when he/she was in charge?
8. Were there times when you got him to quiet down?
9. How often does she speak to you?
10. Are there times when he gets louder?

Take some time with this exercise. Really make a distinction between the natural heroic you and the critic who came later.

If these questions are particularly challenging, or if you are having difficulty consistently turning up the volume on your inner critic in order to hear him as distinct from your natural voice, work on this exercise over time. For example, the next time you notice your inner critic spreading his negativity, immediately try to accentuate and differentiate his voice by making it sound decidedly different from yours. Have fun with this— perhaps you can try an accent (I suggest French—unless, of course, you are French; then try American), or try to make his voice louder or unusual in some way. If you associate your inner critic with a voice that sounds different from yours, soon enough it will become automatic and you will begin to see your inner critic as separate from your inner hero.

Now that you have some distance from your inner critic, the time has come to turn around and come face to face with the abyss of fear, doubt, and loathing he has carved out in front of you in the name of protecting you.

» Facing the Abyss: What Does It Mean?

Fear and doubt are the drugs that your inner critic has been feeding you for years—keeping you feeling safe but hobbled. If you or anyone you know has ever struggled with alcohol or drug addiction, you probably know that one of the keys to staying clean is letting go or giving up control. Letting go of control is, ironically, one of the most powerful things you can do in every realm of your life. That is why we are going to use this method to move through your inner critic. It is an act of faith. When you confront terror armed with faith, you make fear your slave.

As you embrace your lack of control over your inner critic you will rediscover your true power. I call this process "facing the abyss," because it involves you confronting and accepting the possibility that all of your worst fears and doubts are true, or will come true.

How does this work? Let's say, for example, that you have decided that you want to be a singer. Your inner critic may tell you that you are a lousy singer. He says that you have no talent and you will never make it in the music business. Perhaps he tells you, "Pack it in. Go to law school like your dad. Maybe you could do that. At least you have a model for how to be a lawyer. What do you know about being a singer, anyway?"

What are your options here?

- **Option 1:** You can listen to your critic and do what he says, but that will just prove him right. Giving in to your inner critic will strengthen his hand the next time you try to take action on what's next for you. You're not going to do that, so let's look at option 2.

- **Option 2:** You can try to debate your inner critic. This is the approach that most people take, but it is doomed to fail because it is an attempt to use reason to overcome passion (your inner critic, who is born of emotion, is a passionate guy).

This approach can work in some cases, usually when you have some emotional distance from the situation. But we are talking about your life and what's next for you, and there is no way you could or should have emotional distance from it.

Many people believe they can reason their way through their feelings, as if emotions are a nuisance, a distraction to be dealt with like a mosquito. I have had many men come into my office—I must admit, it's usually men—who ask me how they can learn to pin their emotions to the mat, as if they were Hulk Hogan. But the truth is they can't, you can't, and I can't. No one can. The best you can hope for is a truce.

The reason you can't use your rational mind to control your emotions is that your feelings are much stronger than your thoughts. If you have tried doing this you may have had success from time to time, but only if your feelings about something are weak or ambivalent. But when your passions are boiling, your thoughts have little hope. If this doesn't ring true for you, take the following quiz to see how this process may factor into your life:

Quiz:

WHO'S IN CHARGE? THOUGHTS OR FEELINGS?

① Consider your worst romantic relationship. Think about how he/she treated you. Was there ever a point when you knew for sure that you needed to end it? Did you do it right away?

① Yes. As soon as you realized that he/she was wrong for you, you walked out the door—Gloria Gaynor style.

② Not exactly. You went back a few times and it took you a while, but eventually you put him/her out to pasture.

③ You kept going back and back and back until eventually a final straw pushed you to break it off.

② **Now think about someone whom you love, who is close to you, whom you support entirely and wish well (please do not choose your child for this question for reasons that are beyond the scope of this book). Imagine, or think back to, a time when you wanted something that this person had, or you were competing for the same thing. Imagine that this other person got this thing but you did not. How did you feel?**

① You felt entirely supportive of him or her inside and out—you genuinely wanted him/her to get it with every fiber of your being.

② You were generally happy for the person but were a bit resentful or jealous, even if you didn't show it on the outside.

③ You were bitter inside.

❸ **Imagine your boss calls you into his or her office to talk to you about how you are doing at your job. He tells you that you are doing an amazing job. Your work product is outstanding, and you are going to get a raise. He has no complaints about you personally or professionally. However, before you leave he tells you that a couple of people have told him that you can be a bit pushy when you are trying to get things done, and you might want to soften up a bit—but it's not a big deal. On the whole you are doing great. How would you feel after getting this feedback?**

① You would feel amazing—like the superstar that he told you that you are.

② You would feel pretty good about all the praise but would have some difficulty letting go of the fact that people have been saying negative things about you.

③ You would be obsessed with the negative comments to the point that you'd practically forget about all of the praise.

Let's see how you did. Add up the scores (1, 2, or 3) on the three questions from this quiz and look below to consider if your thoughts or feelings are more powerful.

+ +

Who's in Charge? Thoughts or Feelings?—Add It Up!

Total Score 3-4: You are one of the most rational people you will ever meet.

Total Score 5-6: Your emotions can get the better of you at times, but when you don't feel particularly strongly about something you can use your thoughts to guide your path.

Total Score 7-9: Your feelings are large and in charge, not unlike Large Marge.

+ +

In all likelihood you were in either the second or third group here. Feelings are powerful and can, at times, be overpowering. The reason that our feelings are fundamentally stronger than our rational thoughts comes down to one word: time.

As humans, our emotional systems have been around a lot longer than our higher brain systems and are far more brilliant and sophisticated than science has allowed us to understand and appreciate thus far. Moreover, for you personally, your emotions came before your ability to reason. Before you knew how to speak or reason your way into or out of anything, your emotions were there. They are, were, and will be entangled with your ability to think logically. In fact, we can't think logically without our emotions. Emotions are primal, primary, and extremely powerful.

The fact that you can't overpower your feelings doesn't make you "dumb"—it makes you human.

Instead of thinking about how to dominate your feelings or your inner critic you should consider how you can work with them. Don't waste your energy fighting directly with your critic or your feelings. You will lose the fight, and you may even lose your motivation for taking on your next big thing in the process.

Trying to engage your inner critic in a debate is like trying to reason with a person who is actively psychotic. If you've never done this, I don't recommend it. Try to imagine, for example—not that this has ever happened to me personally, of course—that you are a clinical psychology doctoral student working in a hospital and you have been assigned to do therapy with a woman who is in the midst of an acute psychotic episode. If this woman is certain that the only reason you could possibly be in her hospital room is that you are going to clean her radiator, all the talk in the world *will not* convince her otherwise. Trying to get into a logical discussion with her about why you are there will just frustrate you and her and make you wonder why you wanted to get a PhD in clinical psychology in the first place. You might even begin to think that you *should* clean her radiator before you leave her room.

›› Facing the Abyss: How Do You Do It?

Instead of trying to reason with your inner critic, you are going to go through him by facing the abyss.

The way to do this is to accept that everything he is telling you may be true.

Yes, you read that right: Now that you have learned who your critic is and where he comes from, and you have separated from him, I want you to accept that any negative thing he says about you might *actually* be true. You might be all of those terrible things he says you are, and you might never get to do the things that your inner hero wants you to do—I am not going to bother to list them here. Instead, you are.

Exercise:

YOUR STATEMENT OF FEAR

Take out your Statement of Purpose from Chapter 4—if you haven't yet written it, this would be a good time to do so.

Look it up and look it down.

Now I want you to do something that will seem very odd. I want you to write out a Statement of Fear. Come up with every reason you can possibly think of that you will not be able to accomplish what you have written in your Statement of Purpose. Go for it. Let loose. Think of it as Mardi Gras for your inner critic.

Your personal Statement of Fear should include the following information (the first two points should be identical to your Statement of Purpose):

1. Your name.
2. Between one and three things that are important to you. Begin with the words, "I believe in . . ."
3. Two or three sentences about why you will *not* be able to take action on what's important to you. Begin the sentences with the words "I can't," or "I won't," or "I am not able to."

Just as with your Statement of Purpose, your Statement of Fear should be no more than 100 words. Using the Jane Doe Statement of Purpose from the last chapter as an example, consider what this might look like:

My name is Jane Doe. I believe in the power of education to improve the future. I believe teaching children how to be compassionate human beings is the foundation for cooperation and charity. *I can't become a kindergarten teacher because I am a terrible test taker and will probably fail the Certification Exam. This will remind me that I am a failure. I won't keep trying after that. Even if I did pass the test I wouldn't be able to keep up with all of the paperwork because I'm too disorganized.*

After you've written out all of your fears and doubts you are not going to give up in despair—what kind of lousy book would this be if that were my advice?

Instead, embrace the possibility that your inner critic's assertions could be true. You are going to accept the possibility that your Statement of Fear is your future. However—and this is the important point—*you will act as if it is not.*

Let's see how this would play out in the Jane Doe example. Jane Doe feels like a failure. She has tremendous test anxiety, which will get in the way of her taking the Teacher Certification Exam. She is going to accept failing the exam as a possible outcome for her and her future. But instead of acting as though what her critic told her is true, she will act as though it is false. In this case, Jane will act as if she were someone who *is* a good test taker and is capable of—no, strike that—is *going* to pass the exam. This will mean that she will study diligently and do everything she can to ease her worries on the day of the exam—get enough sleep, eat the right foods, and stay present when she sits for the exam (see Chapter 10 for more on living in the present). If Jane Doe embraces the possibility of failure but acts as if she will be successful, the hero inside of her will ultimately prevail.

This is not magic. The reason facing the abyss works is that by facing and embracing your fears you let go of the need to control them. Instead, all the energy you would have spent trying in vain to be in control will go into your next big thing. And then . . . it's just a matter of time.

In the end, avoiding your critic will hurt you more than moving toward him. That may not make it any easier, but it is the truth. Facing your critic is a sign that you are making a choice and taking a stand. You are declaring to yourself that you are moving forward. You are getting on with your life.

CHOOSE »

Now that you know how to approach your inner critic and have accepted that what he tells you might be true, the time has come for you to make a choice.

Deciding on and executing your next big thing is fundamentally a creative process, and you cannot be a creator and critic at the same time. I'm going to say that again to make sure you heard it. *You cannot be a creator and critic at the same time.* To take on both roles is like constructing a building with your right hand while demolishing it with your left. If you are considering trying this, it's a bad idea. Creation and destruction are mutually exclusive. If you want to get to the next stage of your life and start creating something new, go for it. If you want to be a critic, then criticize and tear down, but make no mistake, you've got to choose. So, if you're with me, put down your sledgehammer and pick up your paintbrush.

Exercise:

CHOOSE

Pick up your Statement of Purpose with your right hand and look it over. Study it. Imagine yourself acting in accord with your purpose—living a life full of meaning and joy. Now pick up your Statement of Fear with your left hand and review it. Read it carefully and soak it in. That is also a possible future for you.

Which one do you want?

Do you want to cross the abyss or fall in? There is only one bridge across the ravine and you have to create it with faith and action. If you believe in your vision and in yourself you will pass through to the other side.

Choose what you want your future to be. Do you want it to be like your Statement of Purpose—full of promise, challenge, and joy? Or do you want it to be like your Statement of Fear—replete with doubt, despair, and terror? Whichever one you choose (*please* let it be the Statement of Purpose), take the other one, crumple it up, and throw it away.

Let me be clear here—this is not a quick fix. I am not going to pretend that throwing away your Statement of Fear is a panacea for silencing your inner critic, because it's not. It's a symbol—a sign that you are letting go of the Then You and are committing to the New You. It is a step. It may not feel like much, but it is. Your critic is not as easily thrown away as a piece of paper, but if you keep trying to see and stare him or her down, you will do it. Like anything worth doing, this is a process, and success does not happen as soon as you put your mind to it. In time, however, you will be able to see your critic clearly and manage him. You have begun to pass through your inner critic and that is all you need in order to do exactly what you need to do now: Take action. And what's convenient for you is exactly what's next . . .

It's time to turn the page.

**THE
TAKEAWAY**

1 Your inner critic is the voice inside of you that wants to hold you back and keep you from trying new or different things.

2 In order to move on to your next big thing you must, at some point, face your inner critic.

3 You learned that your inner critic developed to help protect you from feeling helpless or overwhelmed when you were a child.

4 Although your critic has an important role in your life and psyche, he can get in the way of your next big thing.

5 You turned up the volume on your critic by learning to recognize him as a part of you rather than all of you.

6 You faced the abyss of fear by accepting the possibility that what your critic says may come true but began acting as if it were false.

7 You chose between your Statement of Purpose and your Statement of Fear.

TAKE ACTION

Chapter

6

Even when you know exactly what you want your next step to be, actually taking action on it can be a challenge. Beginning a new endeavor is usually difficult for people for two reasons:

1. **They don't start at the beginning**
2. **They are unsure what to do.**

Let's deal with each of these in turn.

START AT THE START »

The very idea of not starting at the start might seem kind of absurd to you. Isn't wherever you start "the start"? Actually, no, it's not. When your mind pulls you into an unknown future because you are anxious (we'll discuss why and how this happens when we talk about Living in the Now in Chapter 10), you may find it hard to commit to decisive action about the next part of your life because any steps you take will not be in synch with where you are now. This misalignment will cause you to stutter, sputter, and stall. How does this work? Let's say, for example, you have realized that you are completely stuck in your job. It has become clear to you (possibly from reading this book) that you are no longer doing work that inspires and challenges you or that is in line with your personal values. It is time for a change. However, there is another part of you that begins thinking about your five-year plan to move elsewhere (closer to home, the suburbs, or a new place altogether). You think to yourself, "Well, I can't start looking for a new job now because I may be moving away in a few years. I'm not going to begin a job search now just to do it again in three years." So instead, you do nothing. Moving becomes daunting so you stay where you are: stuck.

You could have avoided this whole situation if you had taken action from where you are now: stuck in a job that you don't like in the place you live now, instead of three years from now. A lot can happen in three years and if you take action now, a lot *will* happen, but if you sit back and wait because your mind ties you to an uncertain future, not much can or will happen to change things and you will remain running in place instead of moving with purpose.

This is why you need to start at the start.

If this is all a bit confusing, consider how my patient Chuck, the rather angry man you met back in Chapter 2, had difficulty starting at the start and how it got in the way of his taking action.

Chuck

As the therapy with Chuck progressed he came to know himself. In time he imagined a new horizon and discovered his true purpose. After exploring his values and joy, Chuck eventually wrote out his personal Statement of Purpose which made it clear that he was meant to be an entrepreneur. In fact, he was a born entrepreneur but was reluctant to live in accord with his own nature. This was a watershed moment in our work together, yet the revelation of his purpose and path initially brought Chuck more stress than relief.

He struggled with his realization and tried to reconcile his feelings about risk-taking entrepreneurs with his personal experience. A generation ago, Chuck's father, also a natural-born entrepreneur, tried to branch out on his own, but because he had used the resources of his employer to fund and develop his idea, the company that he worked for claimed the patent on his invention. As a result, Chuck's father received only modest financial and professional benefits from his creation. This crushed his spirit and ultimately his family's fortunes. Chuck had vowed not to be a "sucker" like his dad.

After completing his Statement of Purpose, Chuck did not take any action to create his own enterprise. He remained entrenched at the bank and became angrier. About six weeks later, Chuck's boss gave him an assignment that he considered to be beneath him. He passed it off to one of his junior colleagues. When his boss found out, he reassigned it to Chuck. Chuck was no longer able to contain his fury and unleashed on his boss. Somewhat surprisingly, however, this did not end his career or his job. Either his boss was an unusually understanding person, or Chuck was incredibly good at his job, or something else happened that I don't understand, because even after verbally assaulting his boss, Chuck didn't get fired. He was compelled to take an anger management course through his company, but he kept his job.

The next session was the only time Chuck ever cried in my office. He couldn't, he *wouldn't* leave his job. Chuck knew what it was like out there and how hard it would be to get another job. He felt trapped. He didn't want to leave his job but he felt as if he couldn't stay.

His head was in his hands.

"I don't know what to do," he said.

"Actually, you do," I responded. "You were meant to be your own boss, and there is something inside of you that is pushing you in that direction."

Chuck said that most entrepreneurs were just "hacks" who languished in anonymity. "I'm not going to be poor, and I'm not going to be mediocre," he declared. He told me that he had a nice setup: a well-paying job at a brand-name company, a "sick apartment," and he wasn't about to give any of that up. "I don't know where to begin."

"How about at the beginning." I offered.

- -

Do you see where Chuck was getting stuck? He told me that he was not going to leave his high-paying brand-name job or his "sick" apartment, but who said he had to? It is true that he might *eventually* leave his job (which he did), but that could be (would be) years away and actually had nothing to do with what he needed to do at that moment. He was thinking down the line, not in the Now. For now, all Chuck had to do was start.

The same is true for you. If you have stayed with me thus far and have a vision for where you want to go but are having difficulty taking concrete action on the next steps, you are not alone. We just need to get you moving.

Let's assume for now that you have an idea about what you want to do next but are having difficulty moving from vision to action. This quiz is designed to help you understand the impediments to getting going.

Quiz:

WHAT'S IN YOUR WAY?

❶ Spend a moment or two thinking about what you want to do next. Do you feel ready to take action?

① Yes. Nothing can stop you!
② Sort of. You have some ideas about how to start but are just having problems getting going.
③ You have a vision, but feel lost about what to do next.

If you chose answer 1, please put down this book and attack what's next with fury—if you hit a snag, you may want to check in at the beginning of Chapter 7, where we will talk about the process of getting to Next; but for now, stop reading and get on with it!

If you chose 2 or 3, keep going with the next question to see what route would be the best next step for you.

②   If you are having problems taking action, which do you think is the biggest impediment to getting going right now?

① You don't have enough time.
② You can't imagine your next step.
③ You're afraid you're going to fail, so you don't want to start.

If you answered 1, please skip ahead to the next section titled "The Bandwidth Issue."

If you answered 2, you may just be a bit rusty on envisioning the steps you need to take. Try this: First, do the exercises in Chapter 3 in order to get your imagination primed. Go to your play space and take out your play tools in order to get your imagination revved up. Then take out your Statement of Purpose and try breaking down the milestones into even smaller goals. For example, if one of your initial goals was something like "look for a new job," you could break this down into more concrete steps, like so:

- Call Julie and ask her if there are any openings at her company.
- Look in the newspaper and on the Internet for new job opportunities for at least one hour every day.
- E-mail past coworkers and bosses to see if they know of any available jobs.

Now try taking the actions that you write out. For additional suggestions on how to break down your Statement of Purpose into more manageable action steps, try doing the exercise below, titled "Marking Milestones."

If you answered 3 to the previous quiz, please try some of the exercises in Chapter 5 in order to face and pass through your inner critic. If you still feel that you are having difficulties, consider breaking your Statement of Purpose into concrete steps, as suggested in the exercise below, and if that doesn't work, read through the section below, titled "The Bandwidth Issue," as it might help you decide if now is the right time for action on your next big thing.

Exercise:

MARKING MILESTONES

If you created the Statement of Purpose in the exercise in Chapter 4, please take it out now. If not, you may want to consider doing it because it can be a great road map that will lead you to what's next for you.

In order to get you taking action, it will be helpful to break down your general aspirations into more specific milestones. Consider putting down dates for the completion of different phases of your next big thing. How you do this will depend largely on what your personal Statement of Purpose is all about.

As an example, let's break down one of the Statements of Purpose that we looked at in Chapter 4:

My name is Jane Doe. I believe in the power of education to improve the future. I believe teaching children how to be compassionate human beings is the foundation for cooperation and charity. I will develop and deploy my skills as a kindergarten teacher to teach children and ultimately teach other teachers how to teach compassion and charity for other students.

Let's see how she broke this down into more specific steps with milestones and victories marked along the way for her first year:

JANE'S MILESTONES ▸▸
1. Finish my degree in Early Childhood Education
2. Get study guide for the three Initial Teaching Certificate Tests
3. Study for tests
4. Take three Initial Teaching Certificate Tests
5. Pass three Initial Teaching Certificate Tests
6. Apply for teacher certification
7. Search for teaching jobs in my area
8. Get a kindergarten teaching job

This list could have gone on but I suggested that she just focus on the first year; you may want to consider doing the same or at least decide a time frame for you to mark some milestones along the way. The steps on your journey will change as you progress and learn more, but having a structured plan like this is a great way to keep you focused on the initial milestones on the road to your next big thing.

If you were able to break down your Statement of Purpose into specific goals but are still having a hard time taking action on what's next for you, it may be time for you to consider the all-important "Bandwidth Issue."

THE BANDWIDTH ISSUE »

Let's face it: Reality is boring. However, occasionally we all need to deal with it. If you have a vision in mind for what's next for you but are having difficulty getting started there may be a good reason for that. It is possible that you just have too much on your plate right now and you truly can't squeeze another second out of the day. I call this the Bandwidth Issue. Let's see if that's what is getting in your way.

Quiz:

WHAT'S YOUR BANDWIDTH?

Take out a piece of paper or your journal and make a list of as many reasons as you can possibly think of for not taking action on your next big thing right now.

Now, look carefully at your list and answer the following questions:

① In a typical week, how many hours do you feel that you could put aside to begin taking action on what's next for you?

① It doesn't matter. You will make the time for working on what's next for you.

② A few hours here or there.

③ None.

② How will adding one more thing to your already full plate make you feel?

① Engaged and stimulated by the challenge. You need something new, and you need it pronto.

② You will feel more stressed, but you will still be able to manage your many responsibilities.

③ You will be totally overwhelmed.

❸ When you look over your list of reasons not to start taking action on your next big thing, which of the following three statements most closely resembles your thinking?

① Yes, you're busy, but you're always busy. If you wait until you're not busy to get started on what's next for you, you'll never do it.

② You are somewhat busier than usual right now, but you can see a time when things will slow down.

③ You are completely overwhelmed right now and can't foresee it ever slowing down.

Add up the scores (1, 2, or 3) on the three questions from this quiz and look below to consider your current bandwidth.

+ +

What's Your Bandwidth?—Add It Up!

Total Score 3–4: You are busy but committed to getting to Next. Keep reading for some tips on how to get started.

Total Score 5–7: You have a lot going on but might be able to shoehorn a little more into your busy days, but you are not sure. Keep reading below to help you choose.

Total Score 8–9: Your plate is over full right now. You may want to put off taking action on your next big thing. Read the next section in order to decide.

+ +

If you are not sure whether you are ready or not, take another close look at your list of what's in your way. Is it just a laundry list of imaginary, self-imposed obstacles, or are these legitimate commitments of time and energy that will truly derail you in your efforts to get to what's next for you? Remember, your inner critic is always with you, and he is more than happy to furnish you with reasons not to take action on your next big thing. Some of his reasons may be compelling and some of them may not. Only you can tell the difference. You are the expert here, and ultimately you need to decide.

If you're not sure whether or not your reasons are legitimate, suppose for now that they are not. Assume that anything you wrote down is just an excuse, a justification cooked up by your inner critic to keep you safe but stuck. Starting off with this assumption will help to get you moving toward action, and action is valuable in and of itself. Seeing yourself taking action reminds you of your capacity to effect change in your life. You have more potential than you realize, but the only way to get to it is to get to it—no, that's not a typo.

If you have looked at your list and decided that you are too overwhelmed right now, you may need to put your next big thing on hold until a later time. One of the biggest initial challenges to taking action is making the time to do it. If you can't get to it just now because you are inundated by too many responsibilities of the soul—for instance, caring for yourself or others—so be it. Bide your time and make the commitment to do so when circumstances are more favorable. Even if you only have limited spare mental or emotional resources now, it will not always be so.

Deciding to put off what's over the horizon for you is a fair, legitimate, and wise choice. If this is your decision, do not use it a weapon against yourself. Do not look back with regret or self-censure. It is far better to postpone the commitment of taking action on your next big thing than to set yourself up to fail because you are temporarily strained to capacity. Although going through the process of making a commitment and not following through on it is still a form of progress, it can eat away at your faith in yourself and your belief in your capacity for change down the line. There's no need to give your inner critic any more ammunition than he already has.

Cut yourself a break. Some people never do what they were meant to do because they needlessly, and often relentlessly, beat themselves up and question their talent or commitment because of circumstances beyond their influence. Don't let that be you.

THE DECISION TO WAIT ON YOUR NEXT BIG THING »

Deciding to wait on your next big thing does not mean you are giving up. You have learned a lot about yourself from reading this book and have made a considered decision to put Next on the shelf for a little while.

Exercise:

BOOK IT

If you have decided to wait, you are not getting out of your commitment to yourself so easily. In fact, you are not getting out at all. You are putting off, not putting away.

Circle a date on your calendar for three or six months out when you will reconsider your decision in light of the circumstances at that time, so you don't end up throwing in the towel altogether. You can decide then whether or not you are ready to make the commitment to yourself to take action on your next big thing. If that is not the right time, pick another date six months out and reconsider your circumstances then. Don't make the decision now that you will start in six months, because six months quickly becomes nine and suddenly three years have passed. By putting off the date but keeping the question alive, you keep the pressure on yourself not to give up, while simultaneously being respectful of your needs and circumstances.

One note of caution about the choice to put taking action on the shelf: Choosing to wait on what's next until you have more bandwidth is a wise decision, but avoiding it purely out of fear can backfire. Remember, just as there is a part of you—your inner critic—that is afraid of the unknown, there is another part of you—your inner hero, whom we will meet in Chapter 9—that wants to grab hold of the excitement and the uncertainty. Once you begin imagining a new horizon, your inner hero begins to stir and might start mixing it up.

This is what happened with Chuck. In my office he discovered that he was meant to be an entrepreneur but he was afraid that taking action on it would mean giving up all he'd accomplished. This recognition that he was meant to work for himself increased the tension between his inner critic and inner hero and then his boss until eventually . . . *Boom!* He let loose and could've easily been fired. It was this event and the recognition that he could no longer stay where he was that ultimately provided the impetus for him to begin taking action on what was next for him.

THE VALUE OF ACTION »

Suppose you know what you are aiming to do and have some ideas about potential steps to get moving but you are having difficulty deciding which one to do first. The best way to choose . . . is to choose. That is to say, it probably doesn't matter what you decide to do, just as long as you do *something*. If whatever you choose to start with allows you to get started, then it is the right action—for now. Not taking action almost always ends up being worse than taking the wrong course. Moving from thinking to acting is a big step. Once you have passed through that barrier, you can almost always shift gears or change direction to a different horizon.

As you move into Step Six, where you will embrace your process, and Step Seven, where you will learn to defeat the three-headed monster of Passivity, Procrastination, and Perfectionism, you will find that moving forward is ultimately more about flowing with change rather than adhering to formulas. It's not that the order of your actions doesn't matter; it's just that what matters now is that you take *some* action. You can, and should, revise, distill, and adapt your actions and even your vision for the future based on the growth that you are constantly experiencing. For now, doing something—anything—is better than doing nothing. Take comfort in the knowledge that if you have chosen, you have chosen well.

Part of the value of taking action is that, it will remind you that you are capable of taking action. Seeing yourself doing something—looking for work, researching plane tickets, laying the foundation for a building, forging metalwork, writing the opening line to a poem, putting the first circuits together to build a robot, composing the opening bars of music in a song—is extremely valuable, if for no other reason than because you bear witness to the power of your own action. Here are a few suggestions for how to move from thinking to acting on what's next for you:

» Start a Calendar

One of the best ways of encouraging yourself to take action is to write down what you are going to do on a calendar. You may have heard this suggestion before, and if so, there's a good reason you did: It works. Writing your first steps down on a specific date—ideally at a specific time—can help enormously, especially if you tend to have difficulty getting or staying organized. The power of writing your actions down on a calendar can't be overstated. Writing is action; in itself it's taking a step. By committing to taking an additional action on a specific date, you are cultivating tension in yourself. Because as that date approaches, you will begin to feel some discomfort, which can get you moving. Whatever action you plan to take must be written in clear, manageable (read: small and realistic) steps using only action-oriented words. For example: "I will work on my novel for ten minutes on Monday, June 3," "I will dance for forty minutes on Tuesday, April 23 and Thursday, April 25, after work." The language you use should be precise, concise, and measurable, so that you can either build on it or change it as need be.

When you first try this approach, put an activity down on a date in your calendar that is no more than one week away. The first checkpoint should not be so distant that you lose momentum. Whatever period of time you use, you should build in a stopping point so you can assess your progress and plan your next moves. At that point, rest and figure out what you have done. If you write down that you will work on a project for ten minutes per day and in fact one or two of those days you only work for three minutes, or two minutes, or not at all . . . go easy on yourself. Any action you take will bring you closer to what's next for you, and your focus should be about building you up, not tearing you down.

» Making the Time

The first issue that typically comes up when committing to taking action is time; you have a vision, a plan, and motivation, yet you can't imagine how you are going to squeeze one more activity into your already hectic life. I routinely come up against resistance and disbelief when I suggest that this is possible. I have worked through these problems dozens of times with people who have extraordinarily complex lives and schedules, and I can say with unflinching certainty that you can and will make the time to get to your next big thing. You do not need to discover a twenty-fifth hour to get to Next. You just need to set aside the time, which means planning, cutting, and creativity.

The best way to create time is to cut back on nonessential activities. You may not think that you have any such activities, but you do, so let's find them together.

The first place we are going to look for "extra" time is your downtime.

Exercise:

FINDING THE TIME

Instead of looking at a "typical" week let's start by looking at next week. Try plotting out what the *next* seven days might look like for you on a weekly calendar like so:

WEEKLY SCHEDULE						
Sunday	Monday	Tuesday	Wednesday	Thursday	Friday	Saturday
9:00a Wake up	7:00a Wake up	7:00a Wake up	7:00a Wake up	7:00a Wake up	7:00a Wake up	9:00a Wake up
9:30a Get Ready	7:30a Get Ready	7:30a Get Ready	7:30a Get Ready	7:30a Get Ready	7:30a Get Ready	9:30a Get Ready
10:00a Church	8:00a Kids to School	8:00a Kids to School	8:00a Kids to School	8:00a Kids to School	8:00a Kids to School	10:00a Kids Soccer
10:30a Church	8:30a Leave	8:30a Leave	8:30a Leave	8:30a Leave	8:30a Leave	10:30a Kids Soccer
11:00a Church	9:00a Work	9:00a Work	9:00a Work	9:00a Work	9:00a Work	11:00a Kids Soccer
11:30a Church	9:30a Work	9:30a Work	9:30a Work	9:30a Work	9:30a Work	11:30a Kids Soccer
12:00p Church	10:00a Work	10:00a Work	10:00a Work	10:00a Work	10:00a Work	12:00p Kids Soccer
12:30p	10:30a Work	10:30a Work	10:30a Work	10:30a Work	10:30a Work	12:30p Kids Soccer

Sunday	Monday	Tuesday	Wednesday	Thursday	Friday	Saturday
1:00p Lunch	11:00a Work	11:00a Work	11:00a Work	11:00a Work	11:00a Work	1:00p Lunch
1:30p Family	11:30a Work	11:30a Work	11:30a Work	11:30a Work	11:30a Work	1:30p Family
2:00p Family	12:00p Work	12:00p Work	12:00p Work	12:00p Work	12:00p Work	2:00p Family
2:30p	12:30p Work	12:30p Work	12:30p Work	12:30p Work	12:30p Work	2:30p House Stuff/ Errands
3:00p Food Shopping	1:00p Work	1:00p Work	1:00p Work	1:00p Work	1:00p Work	3:00p House Stuff/ Errands
3:30p Food Shopping	1:30p Work	1:30p Work	1:30p Work	1:30p Work	1:30p Work	3:30p House Stuff/ Errands
4:00p Food Shopping	2:00p Work	2:00p Work	2:00p Work	2:00p Work	2:00p Work	4:00p House Stuff/ Errands
4:30p Food Shopping	2:30p Work	2:30p Work	2:30p Work	2:30p Work	2:30p Work	4:30p House Stuff/ Errands
5:00p Food Shopping	3:00p Work	3:00p Work	3:00p Work	3:00p Work	3:00p Work	5:00p House Stuff/ Errands
5:30p	3:30p Work	3:30p Work	3:30p Work	3:30p Work	3:30p Work	5:30p House Stuff/ Errands
6:00p	4:00p Work	4:00p Work	4:00p Work	4:00p Work	4:00p Work	6:00p House Stuff/ Errands
6:30p Fix Dinner	4:30p Work	4:30p Work	4:30p Work	4:30p Work	4:30p Work	6:30p Fix Dinner
7:00p Kids HW	5:00p Work	5:00p Work	5:00p Work	5:00p Work	5:00p Work	7:00p Dinner
7:30p Kids to Bed	5:30p Work	5:30p Work	5:30p Work	5:30p Work	5:30p Work	7:30p

Sunday	Monday	Tuesday	Wednesday	Thursday	Friday	Saturday
8:00p Kids to Bed	6:00p Pick Up Kids	6:00p Pick Up Kids	6:00p Pick Up Kids	6:00p Pick Up Kids	6:00p Pick Up Kids	8:00p
8:30p Kids in Bed	6:30p Fix Dinner	6:30p Fix Dinner	6:30p Fix Dinner	6:30p Fix Dinner	6:30p Fix Dinner	8:30p
9:00p TV	7:00p Kids HW	7:00p Kids HW	7:00p Kids HW	7:00p Kids HW	7:00p Kids HW	9:00p Go Out
9:30p TV	7:30p Kids to Bed	7:30p Kids to Bed	7:30p Kids to Bed	7:30p Kids to Bed	7:30p Kids to Bed	9:30p
10:00p TV	8:00p Kids to Bed	8:00p Kids to Bed	8:00p Kids to Bed	8:00p Kids to Bed	8:00p Kids to Bed	10:00p
10:30pTV	8:30p Kids in Bed	8:30p Kids in Bed	8:30p Kids in Bed	8:30p Kids in Bed	8:30p Kids in Bed	10:30p
11:00p	Go to Bed	9:00p TV	9:00p TV	9:00p TV	9:00p TV	9:00p TV
9:30p TV	9:30p TV	9:30p TV	9:30p TV	9:30p TV	9:30p TV	9:30p TV
10:00p TV	10:00p TV	10:00p TV	10:00p TV	10:00p TV	10:00p TV	10:00p TV
10:30p TV	10:30p TV	10:30p TV	10:30p TV	10:30p TV	10:30p TV	10:30p TV
11:00p Go to Bed	11:00p Go to Bed	11:00p Go to Bed	11:00p Go to Bed	11:00p Go to Bed	11:00p Go to Bed	11:00p Go to Bed

Your weekly calendar may look nothing like this. It's just a sample to give you a sense of how you can do this. You won't know everything you are going to do in the next week—no one does—so it won't be perfect (a word that, hopefully, you will soon learn to hate as much as I do), but it will be what it needs to be, which is good enough to get you started. Once you have plotted out your week, spend some time looking over your week—do you see any windows of time that you can use to get started on your next big thing? Let's look at this person's calendar. He is clearly very busy, working a full-time job and taking care of more than one child, but even he has a couple of small windows that he could use to get started on what's next for him.

WEEKLY SCHEDULE (DETAIL)						
Sunday	Monday	Tuesday	Wednesday	Thursday	Friday	Saturday
4:00p Food Shopping	2:00p Work	2:00p Work	2:00p Work	2:00p Work	2:00p Work	4:00p House Stuff/ Errands
4:30p Food Shopping	2:30p Work	2:30p Work	2:30p Work	2:30p Work	2:30p Work	4:30p House Stuff/ Errands
5:00p Food Shopping	3:00p Work	3:00p Work	3:00p Work	3:00p Work	3:00p Work	5:00p House Stuff/ Errands
5:30p	3:30p Work	3:30p Work	3:30p Work	3:30p Work	3:30p Work	5:30p House Stuff/ Errands
6:00p	4:00p Work	4:00p Work	4:00p Work	4:00p Work	4:00p Work	6:00p House Stuff/ Errands
6:30p Fix Dinner	4:30p Work	4:30p Work	4:30p Work	4:30p Work	4:30p Work	6:30p Fix Dinner
7:00p Kids HW	5:00p Work	5:00p Work	5:00p Work	5:00p Work	5:00p Work	7:00p Dinner
7:30p Kids to Bed	5:30p Work	5:30p Work	5:30p Work	5:30p Work	5:30p Work	7:30p
8:00p Kids to Bed	6:00p Pick Up Kids	6:00p Pick Up Kids	6:00p Pick Up Kids	6:00p Pick Up Kids	6:00p Pick Up Kids	8:00p
8:30p Kids in Bed	6:30p Fix Dinner	6:30p Fix Dinner	6:30p Fix Dinner	6:30p Fix Dinner	6:30p Fix Dinner	8:30p
9:00p TV	7:00p Kids HW	7:00p Kids HW	7:00p Kids HW	7:00p Kids HW	7:00p Kids HW	9:00p Go Out
9:30p TV	7:30p Kids to Bed	7:30p Kids to Bed	7:30p Kids to Bed	7:30p Kids to Bed	7:30p Kids to Bed	9:30p
10:00p TV	8:00p Kids to Bed	8:00p Kids to Bed	8:00p Kids to Bed	8:00p Kids to Bed	8:00p Kids to Bed	10:00p
10:30p TV	8:30p Kids in Bed	8:30p Kids in Bed	8:30p Kids in Bed	8:30p Kids in Bed	8:30p Kids in Bed	10:30p

Perhaps he could fit some time in during these blocks. Remember, getting started is all we're after here. Once you start seeing yourself taking action it becomes easier to do more.

Another strategy is to try to cut down on some activities in order to make the time you will need. As busy as this man is, notice that he watches more than twelve hours of television during his week. If we were to reduce this just slightly, he would have all the time he needs to get started taking action on what's next.

WEEKLY SCHEDULE (DETAIL)						
Sunday	Monday	Tuesday	Wednesday	Thursday	Friday	Saturday
4:00p Food Shopping	2:00p Work	2:00p Work	2:00p Work	2:00p Work	2:00p Work	4:00p House Stuff/ Errands
4:30p Food Shopping	2:30p Work	2:30p Work	2:30p Work	2:30p Work	2:30p Work	4:30p House Stuff/ Errands
5:00p Food Shopping	3:00p Work	3:00p Work	3:00p Work	3:00p Work	3:00p Work	5:00p House Stuff/ Errands
5:30p	3:30p Work	3:30p Work	3:30p Work	3:30p Work	3:30p Work	5:30p House Stuff/ Errands
6:00p	4:00p Work	4:00p Work	4:00p Work	4:00p Work	4:00p Work	6:00p House Stuff/ Errands
6:30p Fix Dinner	4:30p Work	4:30p Work	4:30p Work	4:30p Work	4:30p Work	6:30p Fix Dinner
7:00p Kids HW	5:00p Work	5:00p Work	5:00p Work	5:00p Work	5:00p Work	7:00p Dinner
7:30p Kids to Bed	5:30p Work	5:30p Work	5:30p Work	5:30p Work	5:30p Work	7:30p
8:00p Kids to Bed	6:00p Pick Up Kids	6:00p Pick Up Kids	6:00p Pick Up Kids	6:00p Pick Up Kids	6:00p Pick Up Kids	8:00p

Sunday	Monday	Tuesday	Wednesday	Thursday	Friday	Saturday
9:00p	7:00p Kids HW	7:00p Kids HW	7:00p Kids HW	7:00p Kids HW	7:00p Kids HW	9:00p Go Out
9:30p	7:30p Kids to Bed	7:30p Kids to Bed	7:30p Kids to Bed	7:30p Kids to Bed	7:30p Kids to Bed	9:30p
10:00p	8:00p Kids to Bed	8:00p Kids to Bed	8:00p Kids to Bed	8:00p Kids to Bed	8:00p Kids to Bed	10:00p
10:30p TV	8:30p Kids in Bed	8:30p Kids in Bed	8:30p Kids in Bed	8:30p Kids in Bed	8:30 Kids in Bed	10:30p
11:00p Go to Bed	9:00p	9:00p TV	9:00p	9:00p TV	9:00p TV	11:00p
9:30p	9:30p TV	9:30p	9:30p TV	9:30p TV	9:30p TV	9:30p TV
10:00p TV	10:00p TV	10:00p TV	10:00p TV	10:00p TV	10:00p TV	10:00p TV
10:30p TV	10:30p TV	10:30p TV	10:30p TV	10:30p TV	10:30p TV	10:30p TV
11:00p Go to Bed	11:00p Go to Bed	11:00p Go to Bed	11:00p Go to Bed	11:00p Go to Bed	11:00p Go to Bed	11:00p Go to Bed

For example, if we dropped his TV watching down to just under eight hours per week, suddenly he would have another four hours to get started on a project or something that could move him closer to his next big thing.

Are there things that you might be able to trim back in order to get moving on what's next for you? Look over your weekly calendar and see if you can identify activities that you can prune so that you have enough room to take action.

Try squeezing in just a couple of hours here or there. All you need to do to get started is set aside a little time. Then momentum will take over.

» More Efficiency at Work Means More Time for What's Next

The next place to search for the time you will need to get started is by looking at your job. Most people think they don't have enough time to get all of their work at their job done, so it may seem strange that I am suggesting that you can suddenly discover additional time. If you work smarter at work, you will make better choices and have more time to get going on your next big thing.

Consider how this process went for my buttoned-up patient, Theresa, whom I mentioned in Chapter 3.

Theresa

Theresa was a hardworking professional who felt as if she was running in place. After we broke through her resistance to making lists by using crayons and began crafting a new vision for her, Theresa still found it difficult to take action on her next big thing. She insisted that she didn't have time for anything in her life but work.

I inquired about her schedule, which varied considerably depending on what projects she was working on. At times she worked as many as seventy hours per week or more, including time she spent checking her e-mail late at night and on weekends. I suggested that she leave her computer at work one night a week and answer e-mails in the morning. This was difficult for her to do because she felt that she needed to be "on call" at all times.

Although Theresa initially resisted this suggestion, she eventually tried it. What she discovered was surprising: When she left her computer at home, she was actually more efficient during her workday. Instead of spending time cruising various websites in order to "settle in" to her day, Theresa started her day by checking and responding to her e-mails. She was more relaxed when she was doing this because she was at her desk and could make more organized notes about various tasks that needed to get done, or she could access her files or other information more easily. By making this simple change, Theresa spent less overall time responding to e-mail and felt generally more at ease. This helped her to be more efficient over the course of the day. She felt that she was doing better work because she was more focused, and she had more time at the end of the day to work on her next big thing.

» Work Smarter, Not Harder

Here are six strategies I have used with different patients to help them work smarter, not harder at their jobs, in order to help make more time in their lives for what's next:

1. *On Duty Versus Off Duty:* One of the blessings and curses of the digital era is that you can work from anywhere. I know many people work while they are eating breakfast, talking with their spouses, or vacationing at the beach. Because you can so easily move back and forth between working and playing, it is easy to get sucked into one when you really want to be doing the other. If you can choose what you are doing and remind yourself what you chose, you will be far better off, and more present wherever you are. Doing work when you are not actually at the office may be necessary, but deciding when you are on duty or off duty—and sticking with that decision—can improve your sense of self, help your relationships, and of course, give you more time for your next big thing. Choose one or the other and reap the benefits. It will make you more present and productive in all spheres of your world.

2. *Technology Sabbath:* If you are choosing to take a day off, or a vacation, then do it. A "working vacation" is not a vacation; it's just a change in location. When you take the time away, leave your smartphone at home. Yes, you can do this. Of all the suggestions I have made to my patients, this is the one that gets a lot of push back. You can take a day off or go on vacation without your smartphone. Believe me. I do this myself, and it takes some planning and effort, but if you want to unplug, it is possible and worth it. If you take the technology Sabbath, don't half do it—*do it*! You will find that you are far more rested and relaxed when you get back. This will make you more efficient at work, which leaves more time for you to execute what's next for you.

3. *E-mail Efficiency:* Respond to e-mails once and only once. If you can answer e-mails only when you feel that you have all of the tools (e.g., information, files, etc.) at your disposal to do so, you will save time and mindshare. Otherwise, you are liable to answer the same e-mail in parts, which is less efficient for you and the

recipient. Responding to e-mails with incomplete information simply for the sake of responding quickly will make you uncertain of your response, and will take up more mental real estate and leave less focus for other important things. This can have a snowball effect on your performance and self-confidence, which can make you more dependent on office "face time" and takes you away from time you could be using to do other things . . . like taking action on your next big thing.

4. **Set Concrete Goals:** Set concrete and obtainable work goals each day. Designate time in the morning to decide on your priorities and realistic goals for the day and work toward them with intensity. Once you have achieved your goals, consider how much more you should do and then make a decision about whether staying at the office merely for "face time" or to assuage your guilt is the best use of your time. Use the additional time for working on your next big thing.

5. **Lunch: It's Not Just for Eating Anymore:** Set aside one lunch per week to take action on your next big thing. If it is not practical to take concrete action toward what's next for you during a lunch hour, use this time to write down notes or ideas that will help you make better use of the time that you do have.

6. **Time Swap:** Trade your weekend time for Friday afternoon and Monday morning. If you work from home on the weekend, as many people do, I will bet that one hour of working from home yields less than thirty minutes of actual productive work. Instead, consider swapping the hours you would be working at home for extra hours on Friday afternoon and Monday morning at the office. You will almost certainly be more productive with that time because there are fewer people in the office, which will allow you to concentrate and get more done. The time you save can be invested in what's next.

We have taken away the weapons of your inner critic, made our first contact with your inner hero, and given you the time you will need to move forward on your next big thing. If you are still standing on the edge of taking action you may just need a little nudge to get going. So let's try a little tender-stress.

STRESS IS A GOOD THING »

Yes, you read that correctly. Stress is a good thing. It just needs a new publicist. Stress is not anxiety. It's just a synonym for pressure, and pressure is a motivator. Without enough stress you won't have motivation to take action, and if you have too much stress, you will feel overwhelmed and won't be able to take action. Just the right amount of stress is what the doctor ordered. To get you taking action, you need to find the ideal amount of stress.

Admittedly, this is not always easy to do because it is a moving target, but that's not going to stop you from trying. Right?

» What's the Right Amount of Stress?

In order to find the right amount of stress to get you to take action, you should start with too much—you can always downshift later. The reason to start with more stress rather than less is that it is better to burn out than rust out. Life is a series of overcorrections. You probably won't find the optimal amount of stress your first time out of the gate, but if you start your process by trying to do just a little more than you think you can, you will add some pressure, and who knows? You might just surprise yourself with what you can handle. Here is an exercise you can use to add a little stress to your life in order to find the amount that's right for you:

Exercise:

FILL THE GAPS

Look back at your calendar that you made earlier in the chapter. Find the holes in your schedule for next week and fill at least two of them with actions aimed at getting you to work toward your vision for yourself. This should create some stress and may help to get you moving. Filling the gaps will remind you that you can do more than you think you can. By trying to slightly overwork yourself you will see yourself in new and exciting ways. This may help you realize that you can do more than you think you can, feeding your confidence. And confidence begets confidence begets confidence . . .

›› Overinvest

At the beginning of the chapter, I told you that one reason people have difficulty getting going is that they don't begin at the beginning. Instead they try to start in the middle or end of their process. The remedy I suggested is to bring the focus back to where you are and to take clear and measured steps in order to get going. Staying in the Now, which we will focus on more in Chapter 10, is a critical part of getting to where you want to be. However, if you are having difficulty taking action just by starting from where you are, another approach to get yourself going is to picture your ideas coming to fruition. By choosing to overinvest in your vision at the outset, you can use your imagination to fuel your actions.

Let's say, for example, that through the process of getting to know yourself and your personal purpose you have realized that you are passionate about an idea and feel that the best way to get the word out is to make a movie. You decide that your next big thing is making an independent film.

You have a vision in your mind for what you want to create and how you want to express yourself. Great. You are already several miles past running in place. Now, of course, you have to go about making your film. It would be extremely difficult, in fact, nearly impossible, to go through the Herculean effort necessary to produce an independent film if you didn't truly believe that someone—ideally many people—would eventually see and connect with your movie. However, if you become so invested in the idea that your final product must be a feature-length film with a massive Hollywood-sized budget and wide distribution that will become a blockbuster hit and sweep the Academy Awards, you may be in for a disappointment.

On the one hand, you don't want to become too invested in your vision of the consequences of your creation, because if your ideal does not come to pass as you imagine, it could be devastating. On the other hand, you need to believe in your vision in order to start your process and to persist when the days are long and your patience is short. If you don't have faith in your idea, you may not have enough impetus to take action; but if you have too narrow a definition for success, you risk disillusionment if things don't go as planned. Underinvestment in a goal results in inaction but overinvestment can lead to being ravaged by your inner critic.

Given the choice between overinvesting or underinvesting in your vision, I always advocate leaning toward overinvestment at the beginning of the process and underinvestment at the end. You can pull back the reins of your expectations later on if need be.

It may be useful to think of your vision as the cause rather than the effect of your process. In other words, if you have a goal for what's next for you, hold fast to it as long as it provides you with the energy you need to get started and push forward. Your vision can serve as your inspiration and guide to your process as your first step on the path. However, you must be careful not to try too hard to control the steps along the way, the road beneath your feet, or the final destination. If you find that you are getting stuck because you are too focused on your end result, it's time to pull back. If this happens, try to reboot by drawing your focus to the present moment (we will talk about how to do this in Chapter 10).

Exercise:

OVERINVEST IN YOUR VISION

If you are having difficulty getting going, take out your personal Statement of Purpose that you created during Chapter 4. Read it over at least twice. Now imagine what it will be like to create a life that is aligned precisely with your vision. Picture it in as much detail as you possibly can. If your purpose involves making a difference in others' lives, run wild with your imagination and take it to the extreme. Envision the impact you will have both during your lifetime and one hundred years hence. Now write it out in your journal or on a piece of paper.

Overinvest in your possibilities. Soak in your vision. Once you have fully steeped your mind in a specific vision of your future, let the energy from the exercise propel you to action. If you are not sure what steps to take then, trying using the exercises in this chapter in order to break up your vision and convert your steps into action.

Okay, you're on your way to your next big thing! Now that you know your path and have taken your first steps on it, we need to address what you will do when you hit the inevitable twists and turns that will confront you along the way. In the next chapter we are going to learn about the importance of getting to Next as a journey rather than as a destination.

Let's walk the path together.

THE TAKEAWAY

1 In this chapter we focused on taking action in order to make your vision for what's next a reality.

2 You learned the importance of starting at the start and how to break down your Statement of Purpose into specific milestones to help you take action.

3 You evaluated your bandwidth and decided if now is the right time to begin taking action on your next big thing.

4 If you decided against starting on your next step right now, you marked down a specific time on a calendar to re-evaluate your circumstances.

5 If you chose to get started taking action right now, you learned a few strategies for making it happen, including blocking out the time on a calendar, cutting down on some downtime activities, and making your time at work is more efficient in order to make sure you have enough time available for what's next.

6 You learned that stress is a good thing and a necessary part of taking action.

7 We discussed two strategies for adding stress in order to get you going: filling the gaps and overinvesting in your vision.

EMBRACE
YOUR
PROCESS

Chapter

7

To call someone "results-oriented" is often a compliment in our society: "Justin is really results-oriented; you definitely want him on your team," or "Lisa is a driven, successful, results-oriented businesswoman." In my opinion, though, being results-oriented is overrated. It is all too easy to become overinvested in your results at the expense of your process. If you are excessively devoted to a specific goal, you can have more difficulty recovering if things don't turn out exactly as planned. This is where the inner critic does his deed. People who are hyper-focused on results can be easily stymied when their results do not match their efforts or vision. This disconnect often leads people to become anxious, angry, or depressed. They may even stop trying, which is the exact opposite of what they should be doing. Instead of giving up, they should be digging in.

People who are not exclusively focused on their destination tend to learn more from their journey and have an easier time adapting to changing conditions or unexpected results. Perhaps more importantly, they experience more joy along the way.

This chapter is all about appreciating the journey at least as much as, if not more than, the destination. When you learn to indulge in the ride, you won't want to stop driving when you make a "wrong turn," because, as you'll see, there actually *are* no wrong turns on the way to your next big thing.

Before we go further on *our* journey, let's take a moment to learn about how you have tended to respond to bends in the road in the past. Take the following quiz to find out.

A BEND IN THE ROAD OR THE END OF THE ROAD?

❶ Imagine that you are (or remember when you were) a student and you just got back a poor grade on a test, which you had thought that you aced. After you get over your shock, how would you be most likely to interpret the grade?

① You would treat it as a learning opportunity, study what went wrong, and apply your new understanding to the next test.

② You would see the grade as due to the combination of bad luck and your misunderstanding about the material. Whether or not you would try to learn from the experience would depend on your feelings about that particular class.

③ You would assume that the grade was a reflection of your stupidity or that the class was too hard for you. You wouldn't try harder the next time.

❷ Now imagine that you are looking for a job. You've applied for job after job but nothing seems to be working out. Finally, you get an interview for what seems like the ideal job. You wow the interviewer with your knowledge and charm and are awaiting the inevitable job offer. A week later you find out that it went to someone else. Obviously you are crestfallen, but how do you respond to the disappointment?

① You would think that you did the best you could but figure that something else got in the way. You would keep on trying until you found a satisfying job.

② You would assume that you must have done something wrong and lower your expectation for the type of job you will get.

③ You would assume that if you didn't get this job, you won't get any job, so you might as well give up now.

❸ Imagine that you recently completed a big project at work. You are feeling good about your effort and results. Your boss calls you into his office and tells you that you've done well but missed the mark in some key places. He will help give you some direction to improve on what you've done. How do you feel?

① Disappointed that it wasn't received as well as you'd hoped, but you d appreciate the chance to learn from the process.

② Upset that you aren't done yet but resigned to the fact that you have more work to do.

③ Furious that your boss didn't appreciate all the work you did. Perhaps you'd consider doing a lousy job on the rest of the project just to teach your boss a lesson.

❹ Imagine that you are single and looking to find a mate. You go through a series of dates with different people, but nothing is working out. Then, out of the blue, you meet a person who really excites you. You find the person attractive and fascinating and you have several shared interests. You go out on one date, which seems to go well, but then you don't hear from the person again. What is your reaction?

① You're sad that the other person did not feel that it was a good fit. In spite of the letdown, you are glad to know that there are quality people out there. This inspires you to work harder.

② You wonder if there is something fundamentally wrong with you. You strongly consider lowering your expectations about the type of person who would be interested in you.

③ You think that you'll never find a good match and decide to give up.

Let's see how you did. Add up the scores (1, 2, or 3) on the four questions from this quiz and look below to see if you are more process- or results-focused.

+ +

A Bend in the Road or the End of the Road?—Add It Up!

Total Score 4–6: You are primarily a process-oriented person. You view experiences and disappointments as providing you with the opportunity for learning and growing. That's a rare and good thing. This chapter will reinforce your current point of view and point to additional strategies to help you appreciate the road beneath your feet and ahead of you.

Total Score 7–9: You are more focused on results than process, especially when the results are negative. You probably spend more time than necessary worrying about how negative results reflect on you instead of focusing on how to improve from the feedback. Let's tip your scales toward a more process-oriented approach.

Total Score 10–12: You are overinvested in results and underinvested in process. You tend to interpret negative results as a reflection of your personal flaws. You may retreat from any feedback out of a fear that it will make you feel bad about yourself. Let's change this together. Read on, my friend. Read on.

+ +

Most people tend to be more results-oriented than process-oriented. This makes perfect sense given our culture and educational system. In school we are taught to rely primarily on results: We are judged by the grades we receive on quizzes, tests, or papers. This is all fine and great, until it's not. What happens when we are done with school? In the real world, feedback is not always as clear as an "A" or an "F." How do we interpret the results that are more ambiguous? How do we respond when we do poorly or even "fail" at something? Do we think that we are a failure or stop trying? Unfortunately, many of us—too many of us—do.

IMPRISONED BY NEGATIVE FEEDBACK »

When we are overinvested in results and uninterested in process it is all too easy to think of negative feedback as a prison sentence—an irrevocable indication of failure. We take feedback personally and are likely to believe that the unwanted outcome means that there is something inherently "bad" and unchangeable about ourselves. Who wants to feel that way? Of course, no one does. Our inner critics usher in these feelings of failure so that we avoid taking chances or going out of our comfort zone. And what happens? We shut down. We become less likely to do the very thing that we should be doing: learning, growing, and becoming more confident from our greater knowledge and experience.

But we are going to change that together.

The way to do that is to embrace getting to Next as a process. From this point on, we are moving on. We are going to advance together instead of retreating alone.

To give you a sense of how I have seen this play out, let's turn back to my patient Amanda, who mistook a bend in the road for the end of the road:

Amanda

I had been working with Amanda for less than six months. In that time she had rediscovered her love for making jewelry. She was playing. She had purpose. She was working.

One day I opened my office door and saw Amanda sitting on the couch in my waiting room. Her eyes were bloodshot, and she had crumpled tissues in her hands. Amanda stood straight up and shot into my office. Before she even crossed the threshold she began sobbing uncontrollably. That particular session took place on the eve of her forty-second birthday. Amanda was despondent because she had been thinking of all of the "failures" she'd had in life. She had recently picked up her jewelers' tools and was experimenting with new ideas and creations. She had set a goal of making one new piece of jewelry a day for a week, but some things came up at work and she'd only made two. She said she was finished—defeated yet again. Amanda assumed that her lack of results meant that she was a failure.

But from another point of view—a process point of view—Amanda had accomplished a lot. Through our work together she had rediscovered the joy she experienced from making jewelry. By starting to work with her jewelers' tools again she had reawakened a part of her that desired to create. The fact that she didn't accomplish exactly what she set out to do that week just meant that she needed to come up with a different approach to moving forward, not stop or retreat.

Amanda was initially confused when I encouraged her to appreciate what she had accomplished thus far. As she considered how to celebrate her progress, we considered what changes could be made to her process. By the end of the session, Amanda decided to make two modifications: First, she changed the time when she was going to work on her jewelry from after work to before work. This helped reduce the likelihood that she would feel exhausted or in a bad mood due to her job, which tended to get in the way of her making jewelry. Second, although she still wanted to make seven pieces of jewelry that week, she would not pin herself down to having to make one each day. If she was feeling good and energized she could choose to make two or even three pieces in a day. This allowed her to have the flexibility she needed in case she didn't feel up to making jewelry on a given day. Those were the only changes she made.

By the next week Amanda had created eleven new pieces of jewelry.

- -

What had changed was that Amanda altered her focus from results to process. During the first week she had been entirely locked in on her goal of making one piece of jewelry each day. When that didn't happen, she felt like a failure and wanted to give up. During the second week, Amanda focused on her process and made appropriate changes based on where she was. Process made all the difference. Instead of looking only at the results, she reoriented herself toward her process and what she could do to move forward.

When you open yourself up to process you can more easily appreciate that the road beneath you is always changing. You will be more likely to move with it instead of being thrown off the path altogether.

Now that you are moving toward Next, how will you respond if you don't get the results you want?

Exercise:

REFRAMING

Start a new page in your notebook and make five columns with the following labels:

Disappointment	
Inner Critic's Interpretation	
Inner Critic's Action	
Inner Hero's Interpretation	
Inner Hero's Action	

In the Disappointment column, write down a recent disappointment that you experienced—if you have one that is relevant to your journey, all the better, but for our purposes any disappointment will do. When you write it down, please keep it brief. There's no need to dwell on it.

Be sure to stick only to the facts of the incident—stay away from your interpretation of what happened. We will get there soon enough. Please frame your writing in the first person. This is really important as it will remind you that others may not see the situation in the same way as you do. As an example, let's use Amanda's experience that I just mentioned:

Disappointment	I did not make the seven pieces of jewelry this week I told myself I would make.
Inner Critic's Interpretation	
Inner Critic's Action	
Inner Hero's Interpretation	
Inner Hero's Action	

Next, write down your inner critic's interpretation of the disappointment in the second column. For this, feel free to be more expansive. This will remind you that once your inner critic starts interpreting your disappointments, it's easy for him to get out of control:

Disappointment	I did not make the seven pieces of jewelry this week I told myself I would make.
Inner Critic's Interpretation	I am a failure just like my mother told me I would be. I always do this. I start projects and leave them undone. I have no discipline. I will never be the person I was meant to become. I am a loser.
Inner Critic's Action	
Inner Hero's Interpretation	
Inner Hero's Action	

Now consider what your inner critic would want you to do. Remember, your inner critic is entirely results-oriented and could care less about process. Let's see where his interpretation and guidance led Amanda:

Disappointment	I did not make the seven pieces of jewelry this week I told myself I would make.
Inner Critic's Interpretation	I am a failure just like my mother told me I would be. I always do this. I start projects and leave them undone. I have no discipline. I will never be the person I was meant to become. I am a loser.
Inner Critic's Action	Retreat from further action that will just make me feel bad about myself. Stop making jewelry.
Inner Hero's Interpretation	
Inner Hero's Action	

Now look at this disappointment from a different angle. In addition to your inner critic, whom we faced back in Chapter 5, you have another voice inside of you. That other voice belongs to your inner hero. We will get to know more about him and how to let him guide you in Chapter 9. For now, just know that your inner hero believes in process. Think of him as a kind old soul who believes in you—in your possibility and promise. Your inner hero wants you to take a bite out of life. Imagine what he might say to you to help you interpret your disappointment in a more favorable, and frankly, more helpful way.

Let's see how Amanda's inner hero interpreted her disappointment:

Disappointment	I did not make the seven pieces of jewelry this week I told myself I would make.
Inner Critic's Interpretation	I am a failure just like my mother told me I would be. I always do this. I start projects and leave them undone. I have no discipline. I will never be the person I was meant to become. I am a loser.
Inner Critic's Action	Retreat from further action that will just make me feel bad about myself. Stop making jewelry.
Inner Hero's Interpretation	This is not the end of the road. I have actually accomplished a lot. I have started making jewelry again for the first time in almost twenty years. I am here and I have a chance to do something different this time. I can't change the past but I can change the future by persisting and pushing forward toward what's next.
Inner Hero's Action	

Finally, now that you have begun to open up to your inner hero, let's get you to listen to him more intently. What will he encourage you to do? Try to be as specific as possible in writing down your inner hero's action. This will help you to take action on his counsel.

Disappointment	I did not make the seven pieces of jewelry this week I told myself I would make.
Inner Critic's Interpretation	I am a failure just like my mother told me I would be. I always do this. I start projects and leave them undone. I have no discipline. I will never be the person I was meant to become. I am a loser.
Inner Critic's Action	Retreat from further action that will just make me feel bad about myself. Stop making jewelry.
Inner Hero's Interpretation	This is not the end of the road. I have actually accomplished a lot. I have started making jewelry again for the first time in almost twenty years. I am here and I have a chance to do something different this time. I can't change the past but I can change the future by persisting and pushing forward toward what's next.
Inner Hero's Action	Revise my creative process to make it line up with my current needs and circumstances. 1. Change the time when I make jewelry from after work to before work. 2. Still make seven pieces of jewelry this week, just not necessarily one each day.

Okay, it's all right in front of you. You have laid it out—congratulate yourself.

Now it's time to choose. Do you want to listen to the exclusively results-oriented inner critic or your process-oriented inner hero? I'm certain you know what I'm going to suggest.

Choose and execute.

This can be a hard exercise if you are unfamiliar with reinterpreting disappointments, but it is a critical part of getting to your next big thing. I suggest you use this exercise for new experiences that have the potential to throw you off the scent of what's around the corner for you.

The reality is that you will hit bumps as you go forward. It is unavoidable and actually, from a process point of view, beneficial to you.

Nobody walks a straight path in life. Every single one of us encounters twists and turns as we grow and develop. The essential thing to remember is that from every experience you either win or you learn. Both of those are good things. When this is your attitude getting to Next is a joy, not a chore.

Things rarely turn out exactly as planned. If you can approach all experiences with a flexible process perspective instead of a rigid results point of view, you will come to see obstacles as opportunities and glitches as gifts.

Now that you are approaching your life's next big change as an expansive process rather than as just a specific goal, we will turn our attention to three of the more common "obstacles" that you may encounter on your journey: Passivity, Procrastination, and Perfectionism. Because these three obstacles come up so often, I have taken to calling them the three-headed monster, or the Cerberus (after the three-headed dog that, in ancient Greek mythology, guarded the gates to the Underworld—yes, I'm a geek). In the next chapter we will learn how to attack, rather than submit to, Passivity, Procrastination, and Perfectionism. When you do, you will learn to make the three-headed monster fear you instead of the other way around.

What are you waiting for? Grab your sword and let's slay the beast together!

THE TAKEAWAY

1 You learned that being results-oriented is overrated because you can easily become overinvested in results instead of appreciating your own process.

2 People who are too results-driven can be more likely to give up when they should dig in.

3 People who are not exclusively focused on their destination tend to learn more from their journey, have an easier time adapting to changing conditions or unexpected results, and experience more joy along the way.

4 You learned that disappointments can be helpful when looked at through a process point of view instead of an exclusively results-oriented framework.

DEFEAT
THE THREE-HEADED
MONSTER

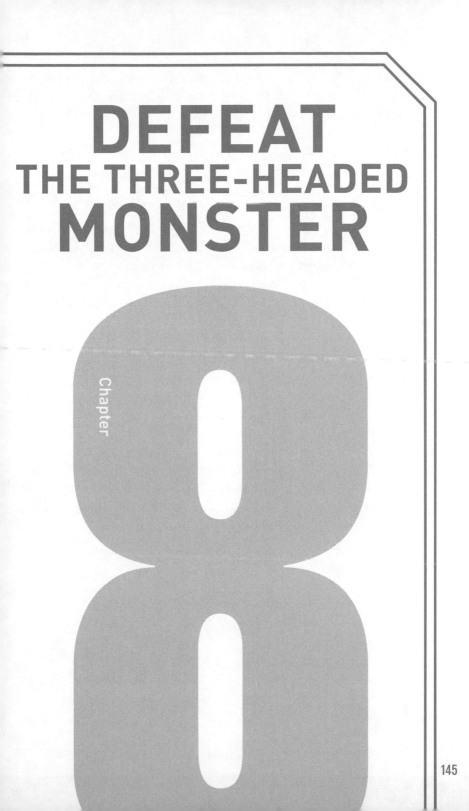

Chapter

8

You are moving with the tides. You are approaching what's next as an ever-evolving process that is constantly developing and expanding. You are learning, growing, and getting to what's next. You have motion. You have rhythm.

Keep riding your flow.

As you sail on toward your future, you will eventually cross paths with Cerberus, the tri-headed monster that can stall or stop anyone when they least expect it. The beast's three heads are Passivity, Procrastination, and Perfectionism. We are going to take some time now to learn about these hindrances and address each one of them in turn. Cerberus affects all of us in different ways from time to time. We are going to learn to kiss this monster on all of his lips (eww, gross!) by taking away his weapons and using them to our advantage. When you are done reading this chapter you will know how to transform Passivity, Procrastination, and Perfectionism from obstacles into opportunities.

PASSIVITY »

The first thing the Cerberus is going to do is try to take away your motivation for taking action. He will tempt you with distractions and tell you that you don't have enough energy to move forward.

Being passive is fine as long as you are choosing to be passive. The problem is when you want to push on but feel you can't because you don't have enough drive. That is the three-headed monster using Passivity against you. We are going to attack him with everything we've got.

Let's start by learning how active or passive you tend to be. Take the following quiz to find out.

PASSIVE OR ACTIVE?

❶ Think back at least one year in time to an important goal that you accomplished. How did you go about approaching the goal?

① You attacked it with fire and fury—that goal should've run when it saw you coming!

② You went about it in a measured way. You figured out what steps you needed to do and accomplished them in a deliberate, though dispassionate, manner.

③ You achieved the goal, but mainly through luck or circumstance.

❷ Now think about something you have done that you are proud of that was very important to you but required more effort than you originally anticipated. How did you *initially* respond when you first realized that it was going to be harder than you thought?

① You rolled up your sleeves (metaphorically) and said to yourself, "I'm gonna get this done come hell or high water."

② You were initially discouraged, but in time you summoned your focus and re-engaged your efforts toward the goal.

③ You decided that the goal was not worth the effort, but you did eventually get to working on it.

Quiz continues on next page . . .

③ Let's say you and a friend were each guaranteed $10,000 but one of you needed to run through a bizarre obstacle course to get it. You knew with certainty that if you didn't do it, your friend would—after all, you could both use the money. There was nothing particularly dangerous about the obstacle course; it was just a matter of running through it and getting it done. How likely do you think you would be the one to run the course?

① You would definitely be the one to do it. You're guaranteed the money so why not have the experience? It might be fun, or at the very least you'd learn something from it.

② It would totally depend on how your were feeling at that time.

③ It would definitely not be you. You'd be happy to have the cash but let your friend do the running around.

Let's see how you did. Add up the scores (1, 2, or 3) on the three questions from this quiz to see how passive or active you tend to be.

✚ ✚

Passive or Active?—Add It Up!

Total Score 3–4: You are active. When you decide to do something you either accomplish what you set out to do or learn from the experience so that you will achieve your goals in time.

Total Score 5–6: How active or passive you are varies depending on your circumstances. When things seem to be going your way you feel more motivated to invest more of yourself, but when they don't, you don't. Consider some of the techniques below to help harness and unleash the active parts of you.

Total Score 7–9: You are more passive than active. You may give up on goals when you feel that you will need to invest more energy than you think you have. You've gone this far in the book, which means that you are motivated to change that. Please use the following suggestions to dig in and go beyond your perceived limits.

✚ ✚

The first two heads of Cerberus, Passivity and Procrastination, are similar because they are only about you. The third head, Perfectionism, involves your inner critic, who may still be hanging around, so we will deal with that a little later. For now, we are going to address Passivity and Procrastination by creating consequences that will force you out of the grips of the monster.

TRIGGERS AND CONSEQUENCES »

All of us are passive or procrastinate sometimes. After all, most of us spend our days working hard, and when we have downtime we just want to relax. The problem is that if we spend all of our downtime relaxing, we can be passive and procrastinate on our next big thing so much that we never get to do what we *want* to do. My solution for this is to create consequences by using our natural triggers to push us into motion.

A trigger is anything that can be used to motivate you, and a consequence is how you use that motivation to propel you into action. Everyone has triggers. It's just a matter of figuring out what yours are and using them to your advantage. Knowing how to use your triggers transforms you from being overwhelmed by your passivity to overwhelming your passivity.

The fundamental triggers that all people have are hunger, safety, and comfort. If we don't have these basic needs met, the consequences can be dire, so we naturally take action on these things first. Once our primary drives are satisfied, we have other triggers that push us forward. These may include love, faith, money, affection, sex, etc. Anything can be a trigger—it just depends on how motivated you are by it. Right now we are going to learn about your triggers and then we will set up some consequences so you can get them to work for you when Passivity or Procrastination come calling.

WHAT ARE YOUR TRIGGERS?

Take out a piece of paper or start a new page in your journal. Make two columns. Label the left column "Values" and the right column "Triggers." Now, look back at your answers to the What Are Your Values? exercise from Chapter 2. Take the values that you selected as your core, secondary, and ancillary values and write them down in order in the left-hand column.

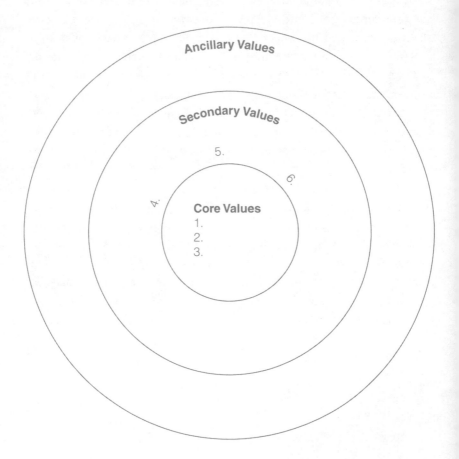

I'm going to give you an example of how this might work. We'll consider the values you selected in Chapter 2.

So, this person's most important values are, in order:

VALUE	TRIGGER
Happiness	
Wealth	
Family	
Pride	
Excitement	
Power	
Health	
Knowledge	
Romantic Love	
Adventure	

Next to each value write down a question about what gets in the way of your values. Your questions should be phrased in one of three ways: "What gets in the way of [your value]?" "What keeps me from [your value]?" or "What makes me [the opposite of your value]"

Here's how this would look for the person's values that we just considered above:

VALUE	TRIGGER
Happiness	What makes me unhappy?
Wealth	What gets in the way of my being wealthy?
Family	What keeps me from my family?
Pride	What makes me embarrassed?
Excitement	What makes me bored?
Power	What makes me feel powerless?
Health	What makes me unhealthy?
Knowledge	What makes me feel stupid?
Romantic Love	What keeps me from experiencing romantic love?
Adventure	What keeps me from having adventures?

In the above exercise, the list of questions in the right column contains a lot of useful information about your triggers. The reason these questions are phrased as negatives (e.g, "What makes me feel powerless?") as opposed to positives (e.g., "What makes me feel powerful?") is because we are all wired to avoid negative experiences. In fact, we are even more motivated to avoid negative experiences than to seek out positive experiences.

If this seems odd to you, consider this thought experiment: Imagine you are walking to work one morning and you see two women. For the sake of argument, let's say the women are identical twins and they are dressed in identical clothing. Now imagine that one of these women smiles at you and the other one scowls at you. Which one of these facial expressions do you think you will be thinking about more during the course of the day? You are much more likely to think about the woman who scowled at you than the woman who smiled at you. You may return to her scowl over and over again. In all likelihood, her scowl will bother you and you may begin to wonder what you did to engender such negativity from her. You may even think about what changes you should make to avoid her scowling at you again. Why might this stranger's expression bother you so much? Because scowling is a negative expression and any negative or bad experience represents a possible threat to your well-being.

We are wired to pay more attention to the negative than the positive, and there is, of course, a good reason for this: If we weren't, we wouldn't be here. Anything we perceive as a possible threat to our well being will stay with us longer, and we will try to address the threat in some way until we feel safe. The question is: How do you use this information to our advantage? That's exactly what you are going to learn to do. You are going to use your natural tendency to avoid threats to help trigger you out of Passivity and Procrastination.

CHOOSING A TRIGGER »

You are going to use your triggers to propel you into action by reminding you of the consequences of Passivity.

Let's look at this list of questions to find a suitable trigger. We could choose any one of these questions. Arbitrarily, let's say this person only works hard when he feels embarrassed. We could choose "What makes me embarrassed?" to propel him into action. To make the trigger effective, this person might tell his friends, wife, parents, and kids that he's having difficulty taking his next big step. If he continued to be passive, he'd be faced with the embarrassment of doing so in front of the people he loves. This would force him to move from Passivity into action.

Remember: I'm just using this trigger (embarrassment) as an example. This may not be an appropriate trigger for you, especially if you are particularly sensitive to embarrassment. In such circumstances, pulling that particular trigger could have other, unintended negative consequences on the psyche. Now back to you. You have ten questions on your list. Simply choose one to trigger you past passivity into action.

PROCRASTINATION »

Now let's turn our attention to the second head of the Cerberus: Procrastination. We all tend to procrastinate when we don't want to do something, but when we put off living a meaningful and joyful life, we end up hurting ourselves in the long run. You can learn how to use your triggers to push you past this obstacle, but first let's see how Procrastination factors into your life. Take the following quiz to find out.

Quiz:

WHAT KIND OF PROCRASTINATOR ARE YOU?

❶ How often do you do laundry?

① Every few days or week. You rarely run out of clean clothes.

② When you've gotten down to your last pair of underwear or socks.

③ After you've worn the same outfits enough times that your coworkers are starting to think that you sleep at the office several nights a week.

❷ Imagine you have been given an important assignment at work. You don't have much going on right now and this assignment is not due for three weeks, but it will involve a lot of thought and effort to get it done. What will you do?

① Start working on it right away to ensure that you will have enough time and mental bandwidth to get it done well and on time.

② You'll probably wait a little while to get started. You've got some other low-priority tasks like Internet shopping that you can use as a warm-up. You'll start the new assignment when you get around to it.

③ You'll probably wait until the last possible moment to start working on it. Perhaps you'll see if you can even get them to push the deadline.

❸ How often do you check your mail?

① Every day or every few days. There isn't much in there that's important anymore, but better to be sure and get out in front of it.

② When you start to worry about getting late charges on your bills or you see the words "Second Notice" on any letter.

③ You haven't checked your mail in months. You don't know what's in there, and you don't want to know.

④ **Imagine that one of the burners goes out on your stove. You have three others so you don't really need to fix it right away. What will you do?**

① Get it repaired as soon as you can—better to have it done than not.
② Wait for another burner to break. You don't need to rush. You'll get to it eventually.
③ Wait until all three other burners break, and even then you might just buy a hotplate instead of dealing with it.

Let's see how you did. Add up the scores (1, 2, or 3) on the four questions from this quiz to learn how much you tend to procrastinate.

+ + + + + + + + + + + + + + + + + + +

What Kind of Procrastinator Are You?—Add It Up!

Total Score 4–6: Whatever the antonym of "procrastinator" is, that's you. When there's something to be done, you get at it fast and furious.

Total Score 7–9: You tend to wait a while to start tasks that will require any real effort but you don't put them off so long that you're overly affected. You might just need a little push to get you started now and again.

Total Score 10–12: You will get things done, but it is usually when you are under threat of serious consequences. You are going to learn how to use this tendency to your advantage. Read on.

+ + + + + + + + + + + + + + + + + + +

If you find yourself in the second or third categories, we are going to use some of the triggers that we uncovered earlier in this chapter to help get you to stop procrastinating and start taking action on what's next for you.

Consider how this worked for one of my former patients: Peter, a fiction writer, who came to me specifically to help him finish his first novel. We used one of his triggers, which was money, to help transform his procrastination into action.

Peter

Peter was a good writer. He wrote for a well-respected magazine and had published several articles in other magazines as well. He had a contract for his first book and things were looking up. Peter had put in a lot of work for months, but now that the deadline was looming he suddenly found himself procrastinating. He just couldn't get himself to write. No matter what he did, he could not break through the morass that was clogging up the wheels of his creative mind. That's when he came to see me.

Once I assessed him, I immediately began searching for a trigger that would force him out of his rut. We used the What Are Your Values? and What Are Your Triggers? exercises to learn more about what would get him moving. As it turns out, Peter was having some financial struggles that were causing stress for him and his wife, who was a graduate student. They were relying on his income to help her finish her degree. These stresses were being exacerbated by the fact that he could not finish his book.

We quickly recognized that money was a primary trigger for him, one that could get him moving forward on his book. Peter and I planned an approach that would affect him financially—enough that the money involved was sufficient to motivate him to work, but not so much that it would overwhelm him or make it impossible to take care of his other responsibilities. We set up an automatic deduction from his bank account of $50 per day to be sent to a charity that supported other writers. (Peter reasoned that if he wasn't creating, someone else should be.) These donations were sent anonymously so he received no tangible benefit from making them (other than the knowledge that he was supporting the arts, of course!) Each day he wrote, we stopped payment for the next day. Each day he didn't write, the payment went through. He missed two days the first week and another seven over the course of roughly three months. The charity got $450, and he got his book done. The trigger worked!

- -

Money is usually a good trigger for people because it can so easily cause stress, which can be transformed into action. Is this an intervention that you can use to get you to stop procrastinating? If so, great. Just make sure you do it thoughtfully and responsibly so that the consequences you face are not overwhelming.

Let's take a look at what makes a good consequence.

WHAT MAKES A GOOD CONSEQUENCE? »

The reason that we were able to so effectively transform this monetary trigger into an effective consequence for Peter was that it met the three criteria for a good consequence: It was sufficient, reasonable, and flexible.

1. *Sufficient.* You want the consequence that you set up to cause you sufficient stress to get you moving. The consequence we created for Peter was sufficient in that it caused him enough discomfort that he was motivated to take action. If, on the other hand, we had decided to contribute fifty cents per day, that would not have sufficiently raised the cost of not finishing his book.

2. *Reasonable.* The consequence that you create should be reasonable. The trigger you choose and the consequence you use need to cause you some stress, just not *too* much stress. The consequence that Peter and I put into place met this criterion for him. If we'd set it up so that if he didn't write on a given day he would have to contribute $5,000 to charity, that would have been way too much. He would either have not gone through with it or, if he had, he would have to endure such stress that it would have eroded the looseness that he needed to create. He probably would have become so obsessed over money that he wouldn't have been able to focus on his creative process. You never want a consequence to be so potentially stressful that it ends up causing more stress than necessary, which is why it must be reasonable.

3. *Flexible.* You want the consequence you create to be flexible so that it can be changed as needed. A consequence that motivates you at one point in time may be insufficient at another. We didn't need to change the consequence in Peter's case because it was pitched at the right level for him. However, that is the exception rather than the rule. More often than not, consequences need to be tweaked to ensure they are working for you as you move forward on your journey.

The automated withdrawal intervention that I developed with Peter also had another factor going for it: it was relevant to his struggle. The automatic deduction from Peter's bank account of $50 per day was sent to a charity that was linked to his work as a writer. This helped him to adopt the following mantra: "If I'm not going to do my work, I might as well help somebody else do theirs." By choosing to support other writers, he was connecting himself to a larger community (even though he donated anonymously), which helped supply extra motivation to keep the work flowing. Making a consequence relevant is ideal, though not always possible. If you can weave it into the consequence, all the better. If not, as long as the consequence is sufficient, reasonable, and flexible, you are well on the road to overcoming procrastination.

Make sure you take the time to consider your triggers and consequences carefully. Finding the ideal trigger and consequence can sometimes take a little effort, but once you do, it can help you immeasurably. It's important to evaluate the appropriateness of the triggers and consequences you chose, changing them as necessary.

Hopefully you were able to find and use one of your triggers to get you past Passivity and Procrastination. If not, keep some of these concerns in mind as you continue to battle against these two heads of the tri-headed monster. Now we are going to turn our attention toward the third head of Cerberus: Perfectionism.

PERFECTIONISM »

You may think of Perfectionism as a good thing, but it's not. The reason you may think it is a good thing is because you are confusing perfectionism with excellence, but they are vastly different. Excellence is a product of deliberate effort and conscious thought—measured practice, patience, and persistence. Perfectionism, on the other hand, is a disease—a compulsion in which your mind circles round and round trying to do and redo a task, working to satisfy an internal critic who can never be sated. Perfectionism is a poison force-fed to you by your inner critic, who more than anything just wants to slow you down or stop you from taking risks so that he can keep you safe but confined. When the third head of the monster has you in his teeth, it can be hard to escape! But you will.

Let's start at the start—where have I heard that before?—and see if and how Perfectionism factors into your life. Please take the following quiz to find out.

Quiz:

ARE YOU A PERFECTIONIST?

❶ Imagine you are a student. You just received a test back and, check you out—you got an "A." Your score was 96 out of 100. Great. How would you feel about the four points that you didn't get?

① You would not be bothered that you didn't get 100—an "A" is an "A." You might be curious about the four points that you missed but only because you would want to see how you can learn from the questions you missed.

② You'd be pleased that you did well but annoyed that you missed anything. It wouldn't matter why the teacher took off the four points. The fact that she did wouldn't sit well with you.

③ You'd feel like the four points that you didn't get were as important as the ninety-six you did.

❷ Imagine that you are writing a play. You feel great about Act One, but Act Two just doesn't feel right for some reason. You can't figure out why—you just know that it's off. Your wheels are spinning and spinning but you just can't make it work. You tell a friend about your problem and she suggests that you move ahead to working on Act Three and come back to Act Two with a fresh set of eyes later. How would you feel about her suggestion?

Quiz continues on next page . . .

① You'd think that it was pretty good idea. You would plan to use Act Two as a placeholder for now and come back to it later. It wouldn't need to be perfect for you to move on.

② You'd think that it makes sense, but you probably wouldn't take her advice because it would be hard to actually go out of sequence even if you were stuck.

③ You would think it was a terrible idea. If you were working on Act Two, you would definitely finish Act Two before going on to Act Three. You wouldn't be able to let go of working on Act Two because you might need to tie it to something in Act Three. Going out of order is just wrong and you wouldn't do it.

❸ Imagine that you are working on a personal project— you are close to finishing it but realize that you need one more piece. It is late on Saturday night and you can't go out to the store and get what you need. In fact, it might be at least a week until you can get the piece. You have something in your house that will work almost as well but you know that it won't be perfect. If you substitute this piece it won't affect the way what you have made looks or works. No one else will be able to tell that you made the substitution. But you will know. What would you do?

① You would use the close substitute, get the project done, and sleep peacefully.

② You might use the close substitute but if you did, it would bother you every time you saw it because you'd know it could've been perfect.

③ You wouldn't use the substitute. You'd wait until you could get the perfect piece, even if it meant holding off on completing the project for a while.

④ Imagine that you are about to give a presentation at work. You look over your slides and notice a small error. It's likely that no one else will notice it but you, and you can make the correction while you are talking. You have a few minutes before you need to present. You can go back and make the change on the slide or you can use the time to prepare for your presentation. What would you you do?

① You'd let it go for now to focus on the talk. You could make the change to the slide later.

② You might change it or leave it as it is. Either way you'd be thinking about the error while you gave your talk.

③ You wouldn't be able to let it go. You'd go back and make the change no matter what—even if it meant being a little late to start the talk. You couldn't give the talk knowing that the error was in there.

Let's see how you did. Add up the scores (1, 2, or 3) on the four questions from this quiz to see if you are a perfectionist.

✚ ✚

Are You a Perfectionist?—Add It Up!

Total Score 4–6: No Perfectionism here. You have a practical and flexible approach toward getting things done and usually don't let Perfectionism stay in your way.

Total Score 7–9: You have some rigidity and Perfectionism that can slow you down or result in your giving up on ideas and goals at times.

Total Score 10–12: Your Perfectionism gets in the way of accomplishing your goals. Keep reading.

✚ ✚

EXCELLENCE VERSUS PERFECTION »

Perfectionism comes up a lot in my work. The difference between striving for excellence and striving for perfection is a lot like the difference between confidence and arrogance. These words are often used as synonyms, yet they are closer to antonyms—we will learn about this in the next chapter when we reclaim your inner hero.

Perfectionism is just a fancy name for a compulsion. Nothing is ever "perfect," and the compulsion to make it so is born of a deep-seated fear. More often than not, this fear will keep you chained to the past or running in place.

When you are not in control of your desires to make something right but instead feel forced to make it "perfect," you are being led in circles by your inner critic. People strive in vain for perfection in the hopes that achieving it will bring them redemption from their inner critic. But it never does. I have seen people strive for the perfect novel, screenplay, economic forecast, legal brief, design, body, face, and relationship. I can say that even if they get what they want, they don't get what they *want*.

Striving to do more and do better is a wonderful impetus if it comes from a place of faith, but when it comes from fear, it yields feelings of emptiness, anxiety, and depression. When I make this distinction, people can usually sense the difference between the two. If you are trying to get to the next big thing because you believe in what you are doing, you may not always be calm, but you won't feel paralyzed either. In contrast, if you are getting stuck because you are afraid that what you are doing is not perfect, it's time to break up with Perfectionism.

THE ROOTS OF PERFECTIONISM »

If you are a perfectionist, changing your ways can seem difficult because you have been this way for a long time; but if you can recognize that, and why and how you are a perfectionist, you are already well on the road. Let's look a bit more closely at where Perfectionism comes from before we talk about how to get you out of this unhealthy relationship with your inner critic.

There are two paths to Perfectionism and they both originate in childhood.

» The First Path to Perfectionism: Conditional Love

The first path to Perfectionism is the result of growing up in a household where love was conditional (we will talk more about this in the next chapter). Love or affection was given to you only if you accomplished or did something right, or "perfectly"—I tell you, the word just makes me snarl. If your parents were only attentive to you when you got the best grade or won the game, or alternatively if they were cruel if you didn't live up to their standards, there's a good chance that you are plagued by some Perfectionism.

» The Second Path to Perfectionism: Disempowerment

Children are all subject to the control of people who are older, bigger, and stronger than they are. If they are lucky, the adults who care for them—parents, grandparents, extended family, teachers, babysitters, and so forth—are kind and seek to do the best they can to make them feel safe, supported, and loved. Other kids have experiences with adults who are less careful, or perhaps, unfortunately, even malicious. Everyone has experienced difficulties and disappointments in childhood that left them feeling vulnerable to one degree or another. One of the ways that many children cope with the experience of vulnerability is by seizing on the fantasy that they, and not their caregivers, are all-powerful beings, in full control of their destinies (the book *Where the Wild Things Are* by Maurice Sendak is the perfect example of this type of fantasy).

Although this is an extremely common childhood fantasy that can bring relief at times to children who feel disempowered, sometimes this wish for control becomes an overused tool. The child then tries to make his or her fantasy of control match their reality, which they cannot fully do. The result is . . .

You guessed it: Perfectionism—the compulsion to make things perfect so that you feel that you are in control of your world. Although the specific content of this wish changes throughout the lifespan, the basic idea remains the same. Your inner critic will help you come up with a rule that, if you follow it, will make everything okay. Children express this to themselves in statements such as: "If I can just say or do the right thing, Mommy will be happy," or "If I can just act the right way, no one will be mad at me," or "If I am a good boy, nothing bad will happen." In adolescence, this can turn into ideas like: "If she will like me, everything will be fine," or "If I get the lead in the school play, all will be right with the world." In adulthood, these ideas become statements like "I have to have the perfect _____ (fill in blank) in order to be happy or loved."

Now that you are moving on to what's next for you, it's time to re-examine these statements and see them as vestiges of another time that are holding you back. The time has come to kick Perfectionism to the curb and take action on your next big thing. So let's do it!

DEADLINES »

One of the best ways to rid yourself of Perfectionism is by simply giving yourself a firm deadline. If you are a perfectionist working under a hard deadline imposed by someone else but you don't feel that what you have done is "perfect," you are forced to make a hard choice between two necessary imperfections:

- Blow the deadline, which would make you "imperfect."
- Keep the deadline, but let go of the notion of what's "perfect" in order to do so.

I have found the deadline strategy to be quite helpful because it forces you to appreciate truth about perfectionism, which is that nothing is perfect. The structure of a deadline encourages you to get things done instead of done "perfectly." Let's put this strategy into action together.

DEADLINES AND PERFECTIONISM

If you completed the exercise in Chapter 6 called Marking Milestones, please pull it out. If not, you may want to do it now. We are going to take the different milestones that you broke out from your personal Statement of Purpose and put them on a schedule. Doing so will help force you out of Perfectionism.

As an example, let's look back at the milestones that we used in Chapter 6 for my patient who wanted to become the best kindergarten teacher she could be. Here were the next steps in her journey:

1. Finish my degree in Early Childhood Education

2. Get study guide for the three Initial Teaching Certificate Tests

3. Study for tests

4. Take three Initial Teaching Certificate Tests

5. Pass three Initial Teaching Certificate Tests

6. Apply for Teacher Certification

7. Search for teaching jobs in my area

8. Get a kindergarten teaching job

What we did with these different milestones was put a few of them on a calendar with specific dates over the following three months that were reasonable given her needs and commitments. I suggest you do the same.

After you put these milestones on a calendar, give a copy of it to someone else and ask them to check in on you. This is very important because having someone else know that you are potentially blowing a deadline will force your hand. If no one but you knows you have a deadline, you can easily shift it out of convenience, which defeats the purpose of the forced choice.

Admittedly, this strategy does not work for everyone. I have had patients for whom the pressure of the deadline did not discourage their Perfectionism but instead aggravated it, which resulted in them shutting down altogether. These patients have said things like, "Well, if I can't do it perfectly by then I'm not going to do it at all!"

If you scored in the higher end (10–12) on the Are You a Perfectionist? quiz, you might find that this won't work for you. If you try it and it doesn't work, it's okay. You may want to consider rereading Chapter 5 to learn about your inner critic or Chapter 7 to learn how to embrace process over results. If this still doesn't help, you may want to seek out help from a therapist who can help you understand the specific roots of your Perfectionism and assist you in forging a path ahead.

Perfectionism is a tricky disease. I hope that some of these strategies helped you to cure it, and that the other ideas and exercises in this chapter worked to help defeat, or at least tame, the Cerberus of Passivity, Procrastination, and Perfectionism.

If you have done this, there is just one more rite of passage for you before you re-emerge as the New You. It is time for you to open yourself up to a part of you that may have been silent for too long.

It is time to reclaim your inner hero.

THE TAKEAWAY

1 In this chapter you faced the three-headed monster of Passivity, Procrastination, and Perfectionism.

2 You learned how to identify your personal triggers and how to use them to create consequences to overcome and overwhelm the first two heads of the three-headed monster: Passivity and Procrastination.

3 You considered how Perfectionism plays a role in your life.

4 You discovered the roots of Perfectionism.

5 You learned how to use deadlines to help you get past Perfectionism.

PART

III

Walking Your Path

RECLAIM
YOUR INNER
HERO

Chapter

9

Getting to the next place in your life never goes according to plan. There will be twists and turns—even experiences that you would have once considered "disappointments," or even "setbacks." You now know these are just opportunities that are a part of your process. You are miles from running in place. You have greater knowledge and more tools; you have faced the road of trials, taken action, and moved past the three-headed monster of Passivity, Procrastination, and Perfectionism. This is all amazing progress, and hopefully you feel proud of how far you've already come—but if you don't, there's probably a good reason: You've forgotten how.

It's time to remember—to honor—to reclaim the hero who has been inside of you since birth.

A HERO IS BORN »

You were born pre-equipped with an instinct for self-preservation. The impulse to avoid harm or death is fundamentally optimistic because, by definition, it assumes two things:

1. There will be a future
2. You want to be a part of it

Actually, self-preservation also implies a third thing: that the future will be good. After all, who would want to persist in life if what was coming next was going to be worse than the past? In short, your instinct to preserve yourself is not just a drive to survive but a drive to thrive—to value and believe in yourself and your possibilities—to be the hero in your own journey.

I can imagine that you may be looking at this with a skeptical eye. You may be wondering, If I was born to be an optimist and a hero, why don't I feel optimistic or heroic?

In spite of our naturally life-affirming tendencies, many of us go through life experiencing emptiness and pain, without ever loving ourselves—with little hope for the future; we carry the belief that the world is a closed and frightening place and that we should be fearful of what's around the corner. Many of us, through overt or subtle training, take in the message that we are not acceptable, not worthy, or not good enough to deserve love from others or even ourselves.

In order to get to your next big thing you must discover—that is, rediscover, your inner hero. Ultimately, it is he or she who will pull you through. Your inner hero is the part of you that believes—in you, in possibility, and in what's next for you.

Let's honor your heroic self by learning what I believe is ultimately the most important lesson you can ever learn: how to love yourself.

LOVE THYSELF »

If the idea of loving yourself seems unfamiliar to you it is because you don't know how to do it. There may be a good reason for this: You have been trained *not* to do it.

When you go through school you learn much more than the information in the textbooks. You learn how to learn and how to get feedback from other people. You become trained to receive responses from authority figures, often in the form of grades, that tell you how you are learning—how you are doing. The further you go in school, the more you rely on other people for praise or criticism, and the further you get from trusting your own judgment for feedback about how you are doing. Over time we become dependent on external validation, and without it, it is easy to give in to your inner critic when the going gets tough.

As you continue on your path from running in place to moving with purpose, you will need something more to help you along your way when the days are long and your next big thing seems far away. Facing your inner critic is necessary but not sufficient because when he is no longer running the show, someone else needs to step up and take over. To get to your next big thing you will need to get in touch with the hero inside of you—and there's only one way to do that: to learn to love yourself through and through: cuts, scars, and all.

» Getting at the Truth

Before you start reconnecting with the hero that's been waiting inside of you all along, let's take a quiz to see how this is all sitting with you.

Quiz:

WHAT'S SELF-LOVE GOT TO DO WITH IT?

❶ When you read the words "Self-Love," how do you feel?

① Fine or good.

② Sort of uncomfortable, like someone just told an inappropriate joke in front of your parents.

③ Nauseous or disgusted.

❷ Imagine a friend of yours told you that she has been working hard to learn to love herself. What would you think?

① Good for her. She is growing and getting healthy.

② That sounds pretty good, but you would worry that she wouldn't become self-centered and forget where she comes from.

③ You would think that your friend has been listening to a lot of shrink-talk nonsense.

❸ Picture someone who loves himself or herself. What do you imagine that person will be like?

① Quietly confident

② Bold and maybe a little brash but fundamentally self-assured.

③ Arrogant and disrespectful.

Let's see how you did. Add up the scores (1, 2, or 3) on the three questions from this quiz and look below to consider how you feel about the idea of self-love.

What's Self-Love Got to Do With It?—Add It Up!

Total Score 3–4: You probably already love yourself and feel comfortable in your own skin, but you knew that already, didn't you?
Total Score 5–6: You are on the path toward loving yourself but you occasionally doubt whether loving yourself is healthy or "right."
Total Score 7–9: Self-love is either a foreign concept that you have never considered, or you have thought about it and the idea of it makes you sick.

If you are in the second or third group, you are in the majority, which means that I have some explaining to do. Whenever I bring up the idea of self-love to my patients for the first time, they tend to feel one of three things: skeptical, uncomfortable, or angry. I have wondered about this for a long time: Why is it that self-love tends to engender such negative reactions? It's not like I'm trying to bring back polio. I'm promoting self-love! What could be more natural than that?

» Self-Love Versus Narcissism

There are two reasons that I get so much pushback when promoting the idea of self-love. The first is that people often confuse the idea of self-love with narcissism, yet the two could not be more different. Self-love is loving who and what you are. Full stop. Nothing more. Nothing less. This can be a strange concept if it is not something you have done or experienced before. It does not mean declaring how great you are from the mountaintop; nor does it in any way suggest that you have the right to trample on the feelings or rights of others because you are somehow more important than them. People who truly love themselves are not narcissists. They are neither greedy nor cruel. They are giving, gentle, and kind.

The difference between self-love and narcissism is similar to the difference between confidence and arrogance, which I mentioned earlier. These two words, which are often mistakenly linked, are closer to antonyms than synonyms. Arrogant people, who do not love, or even really like, themselves, are deeply insecure. They have profound doubts about their self-worth. In an effort to overcome these feelings they promote themselves at others' expense. Arrogance is loud, aggressive, and overpowering. It comes from self-loathing, not self-loving.

People who love themselves are calm, consistent, and confident. They do not need to tear others down to raise themselves up. On the contrary, they use the light inside of them to inspire and promote others.

LESSONS OF LOVE »

The second reason that people resist loving themselves is that they were not taught how to do it. In some cases, they may have been taught *not* to do it.

Although you started out loving yourself, believing in yourself, and having faith in your future, somewhere along the way you got distracted, confused, and lost. This is why you got stuck in the first place. It's time to change that—to reclaim your birthright: to be the hero in your own life.

If you don't love yourself, where do you start? At the start, just the way you did before. Before we get to the techniques that will put you on the path toward loving yourself, let's begin by learning about what happened to your natural inclination for self-love so that we can make sense of why it may not be your dominant impulse any more.

» What Does Love Mean to You?

In order to get a better understanding of what it means to love yourself we first need to know what love means to you. You may not realize it, but you learned a lot about how to love from your family. If as a child you took in the message that you didn't deserve love or that loving people means to put them down, withhold affection, or even harm them, then the very idea of loving yourself can become distorted or even taboo. If you don't have a healthy model for giving and receiving love in your family, it can be confusing or difficult to learn how to love yourself.

Consider how your parents expressed love and affection for each other and to you and your siblings.

- How did they promote feelings of love between you and your brothers or sisters?
- Was love expressed through words?
- Did your father tell you he loved you or did he show you this through his actions?
- Did your mother demonstrate her love by going out and earning a good living to support you?
- Was love expressed through doing things together?
- Was love a scarce resource?
- Was love rationed?

Exercise:

THE MEANING OF LOVE

For this exercise we are going to consider how love was expressed in your family when you were younger. Write down ten words that describe how love was expressed in your family of origin. This may seem a bit unfamiliar if you don't spend much time thinking about this, but it is essential to bring this to mind, not just to help you love yourself but for the next stage in all of your relationships. When you know what love means to you, you can make better choices about how to express it or ask for others to express love toward you. To help you along, here are some examples of lists from four separate people with whom I worked in the past, all of whom grew up in very different households:

1. **Patient 1:** Abundant, active, encouraged, unconditional, promoting/ supporting each other, healthy, good boundaries, joyful, spending time together

2. **Patient 2:** Cold, unexpressed, functional, conditional (based on my grades), worried, fearful, panicked, controlling

3. **Patient 3:** Rarely expressed, only when my mom was drinking, rationed, mainly for my brothers, absent, narcissistic, doled out when I was a "good girl"

4. **Patient 4:** Dysfunctional, random, physical, grand gestures and presents, withdrawn, intermittent, furious, overprotective, uninterested

---

Do any of these words or phrases sound familiar to you? Were any of these patients' experiences with love similar to yours? Take some time to think about the words that best describe the way love was expressed in your childhood home. For better or worse, this was your model for what love means and there is no way around it. If you don't like the way love was expressed in your family of origin it doesn't mean you are doomed to repeat it, just that you need to create a new model for love.

That model starts with you.

›› How Do You Love Yourself?

You may wonder why your new model for love needs to start with you. Why can't it start with loving someone else? Think about it this way: Have you ever been on a plane and watched the flight attendant give the safety demonstration? What does he or she tell passengers who are traveling with young children to do in the event of an emergency? Although it goes against their parental instincts, parents are told to put their oxygen masks on themselves first and then help their children. The reason for this instruction is that if the parents are breathing properly they are more likely to be able to help their children with their oxygen masks than if they themselves are struggling for breath.

It is the same way with love.

Only a person who loves himself or herself first can give love freely to someone else. If you feel loved you know that there is plenty of love to go around. And if you love and believe in yourself, you will have the faith you need to see yourself through the dark times and on to your next big thing.

Loving yourself is not easy if no one has taught you how to do it, but it is not impossible either. Learning to love yourself is not like teaching yourself how to drive or knit or even speak a new language. It is an emotional process that takes time, practice, and repetition. To learn to love yourself you must start small and build from there.

So how do you love yourself?

Well, I'm glad you asked. You do it in the same way you might show love for someone else: by embracing and celebrating the one you love: you.

» Embrace Your "Imperfections"

Loving yourself starts with appreciating yourself—not parts of you, but *all* of you. That is why loving yourself is as much about your "imperfections" as it is about your "perfections" (whatever those are).

There has never been, nor will there ever be, another you. When you stop to think about it, the odds against you being born were infinitesimally low. Considering all the barriers out there to your existing at all, your life is a miracle. In order to take advantage of this gift you need to embrace every single part it. Each piece of you is essential because, well, it is a part of you. We are all pieces of beauty, grime, grace, failure, triumph, and fault— if you can embrace these parts of yourself you can give honor and meaning to the miracle of your existence. The parts of you that are "different" are gifts to be shared, not shames to be hidden. When you appreciate your uniqueness, you behold your beauty.

I have often heard people say that the reason they can't love themselves or are having a hard time finding a healthy relationship is because of their imperfections. They labor under the false notion that if they could just make themselves "perfect" or "more perfect" in some way, they would be able to love themselves and find someone to love them. If you have ever told yourself that if you could just . . . lose that weight, get rid of this, shape that, sculpt this, earn that, or own this . . . then you will somehow be worthy of love, you know exactly what I'm talking about. These are misguided wishes and illusions—cousins of Perfectionism, the third head of the three-headed monster, which we talked about in the last chapter. These fantasies are the very antithesis of self-love.

That's not the road we are going down because it will lead you in circles. Instead, you are going to learn to love yourself the only way you truly can: by starting with your "imperfections."

Exercise:

RETHINK YOUR "IMPERFECTIONS"

Take out your notebook or a piece of paper and make two columns. Label the left column *My "Imperfections,"* and the right column *My Inner Hero's Interpretation.* In the left column write down up to ten things about yourself that you don't particularly like or value—your "imperfections." Be specific. Are they physical attributes? Thoughts you have? Things you do or have done in the past? What are some of your "imperfections"?

Here's an example of what one of my patients wrote down several years ago:

MY "IMPERFECTIONS"	MY INNER HERO'S INTERPRETATION
I need to lose 20 lbs.	
I'm bad with money/need to save	
I'm not generous	
I get jealous easily	
I drink too much	
My scar	
I am lazy	

It may not feel great to write down your "imperfections," but at least they are out there so now your inner hero can help you deal with them. Look at each item on your list and write down one way of reinterpreting the negativity.

First see if you can identify the positive aspects of these "imperfections." You can also think of these parts of yourself as works in progress, rather than negative, unchangeable attributes. You are trying to develop some tools in order to appreciate who and what you are. This doesn't mean that you need to celebrate something that seems particularly bad or harmful, but there's usually more than one way to look at these parts of you. This may not be easy to do on your first pass, but with some practice you will get used to it.

Is it possible to think about these qualities in a different way? Perhaps you can devise a way to share or transform these parts of yourself to help those around you. Sometimes your "imperfections" can even be your launching pad for your next big thing when you learn to embrace and celebrate them.

Here is what the patient I mentioned before wrote down:

MY "IMPERFECTIONS"	MY INNER HERO'S INTERPRETATION
I need to lose 20 lbs.	I want to lose this weight for me and am in the process of making this happen. Losing this weight will not suddenly make me loveable but it will feel good to know that I set a goal and accomplished it. I am going to connect with my friends who feel the same way so that we can get closer and healthier together.
I'm bad with money/need to save	I don't earn enough to save much but I can use this feeling to help me at least become more aware of how I spend my money, which is a good step in the right direction.
I'm not generous	While I can be more generous with my money, I give where I can. I helped my friend who was going through a bad breakup recently and that was a different kind of generosity.
I get jealous easily	When I get into relationships I feel very attached very quickly. That is a good thing and reflects well on my capacity for love. I can do more to increase the good parts of this and try to reduce the fears that I have that he will leave me.
I drink too much	I can still cut back on this, but have been doing better this year. The holidays are tough but I accept that this is a process and will continue to improve in this way.

My scar	My scar is a tough one for me. Most of the kids growing up made me feel ugly for having the scar, which has made me self-conscious about it, but Ted [ex-boyfriend] said he thought it was sexy, which means that other men might feel this way. I need to appreciate it as a marker of something special about me.
I am lazy	I do tend to avoid getting new work at my job but that's really because I need a new job. When I am engaged and interested like I was with my blog I am not lazy at all.

This may be unfamiliar territory for you, and if so—that's good. It means you are changing and growing, taking on the challenge of learning to love yourself and embracing the heroic you. That's a big step and one worth celebrating. Speaking of which, the next way you are going to show yourself love is by learning to celebrate your victories.

CELEBRATE YOUR VICTORIES »

When you want to express your appreciation for someone, you celebrate them. For example, we celebrate people we love with birthday parties and weddings; from one point of view even funerals are a kind of celebration of a person's life. This is the second way you are going to show yourself some love: through celebrating your victories.

I want to be clear that I am not just referring to the obvious victories—the ones that everyone can see (external victories), but also the ones that only you can see and appreciate (internal victories).

You may already be celebrating your external victories, and if so, good for you. Those are the easy ones—the low-hanging fruit. Because of how we learn to receive feedback in school we typically only celebrate or even recognize victories that are clear, definable, and acknowledged by authority figures such as parents, teachers, or bosses. These victories are important, but they are only part of the picture. Learning to love yourself means celebrating and recognizing external victories as well as internal ones, which may have nothing to do with the feedback you get from the outside world.

Positive feedback is important because it keeps you going, and it validates your experience. Seeing yourself making progress reminds you of your capacity to do more and get to your next big thing. Identifying and acknowledging victories can be challenging, especially if you have not been taught how to do it, but it is essential for getting to what's next for you. These victories are there if you look for them. Recognizing your triumphs will allow you to continue moving forward with confidence in yourself.

A win is a win is a win, but only if you count it as a win. If you open your eyes to your progress you will see more possibilities that lie ahead. You will believe in and appreciate yourself in new ways when you see what you can do. Confidence feeds on itself. The more confident (remember: not *arrogant*, but *confident*) you are, the more likely you are to take risks and invest yourself in your future.

You are not alone in your struggle. Consider how one of my patients, Reggie, struggled to recognize and celebrate a vital internal victory along his personal journey to what was next for him.

Reggie

Reggie was a twenty-seven-year-old single man who worked for an Internet media company. He came in to meet with me because of anxiety at work and in his personal relationships. Reggie regularly wrote articles for his company's website. He was extremely critical of his own writing, despite the positive feedback he received.

Unlike many people I have worked with, Reggie imagined and took action on his next step long before he crossed the threshold of my office. He knew exactly what he wanted to do and how he wanted to do it.

But he was terrified.

Reggie wanted to publish a novel. He had completed a manuscript more than a year before he came to meet with me. Reggie had worked hard on his novel but kept it in his proverbial desk drawer out of fear that someone might see it and not like it.

Reggie's boss, Andrew, had been a successful writer. He was well connected in the publishing world. Reggie told me that he had once mentioned his novel in a casual conversation with Andrew, who offered to read the manuscript. Now Reggie was stuck. On the one hand he recognized that this was an amazing opportunity, but the idea of having his work critiqued by his boss, whom he respected tremendously, was paralyzing.

Reggie's process became a classic showdown between fear and faith. If he were to choose to run for cover and withhold his novel from Andrew and everybody else, fear would claim victory. If he were to choose to move forward into the void by revealing his work, then faith would win the day.

Reggie told me that it wasn't ready yet and he didn't want to do it. I shined the light on his ambivalence. I reminded him that it was he who let Andrew know that he had a completed manuscript (his words). By casually revealing this information Reggie was trying to gauge Andrew's interest in his writing. He also chose to bring it up to me in session.

I tried to get him to explore different ways of giving his work to Andrew that did not feel overwhelming to him. We had one session where he outlined a series of small steps toward accomplishing this goal, but it felt like too much, so he decided to let go of it for a while.

We ended up moving off of this topic for a few weeks because something else had come up. During a session approximately three weeks later, while in the middle of an unrelated story, Reggie said something offhandedly about how he was annoyed with Andrew for not getting back to him about his manuscript.

"What?" I said. "You gave it to him?"

"Yeah, like three weeks ago, and he hasn't said anything to me about it. He's probably trying to figure out how to tell me not to quit my day job."

I was floored. Not because he had the courage to deliver the manuscript—that was great, but it wasn't the point. Reggie was declaring defeat when he'd already won. The fact that he had overcome his fears about giving Andrew his novel was the victory, not Andrew's reaction to it, which, incidentally, was at that point still unknown.

He had an impressive internal victory—a triumph over fear, yet he refused to claim it. Instead, Reggie thought he'd lost.

I didn't understand how he'd missed it until I realized that he didn't know how to recognize or celebrate his victories.

- -

Does anything in Reggie's story resonate with you? Do you ever overlook your internal victories or even mistake them for defeats?

That's going to change. We are going to learn how to recognize and celebrate your victories along your path.

MARKING YOUR VICTORIES

If you did the Marking Milestones exercise in Chapter 6, please take it out now. If not, you may want to consider doing it because it can help you take action and acknowledge your milestones and victories on your journey.

Next to each milestone that you wrote down, indicate in parentheses whether it is an internal or external victory, or just a milestone indicating progress along your path.

As you go through this exercise, try to expand your definition of a victory by thinking about events that other people can see and appreciate (external victories) as well as experiences that perhaps only you can know about (internal victories). Remember to focus on things that are both inside and outside your influence. For example, Reggie's huge internal victory was that he gave his manuscript to his boss. His true victory had nothing to do with Andrew's reaction, which he could not control. Instead, the milestone and victory were about his triumph over his fear. I call this an internal victory because only Reggie could appreciate the magnitude of this personal achievement. An example of an external victory for Reggie would be getting his first novel published, because that would be an experience that most people could see and recognize.

As another example, let's look back at the milestones that we used back in Chapter 6 and see how my patient (Jane) defined each of these milestones as personal triumphs that she labeled as either internal or external victories:

1. Finish my degree in Early Childhood Education (external victory)
2. Get study guide for the three Initial Teaching Certificate Tests (internal victory)
3. Study for tests (milestone)
4. Take three Initial Teaching Certificate Tests (internal victory)
5. Pass three Initial Teaching Certificate Tests (external victory)
6. Apply for Teacher Certification (milestone)
7. Search for teaching jobs in my area (milestone)
8. Get a kindergarten teaching job (external victory)

Notice that some of Jane's milestones, such as finishing her bachelor's degree, were more clearly external markers that most people would recognize as triumphs, but others were less explicit. For example, Jane had a lot of test-taking anxiety, so buying the study guides for her certification test was a personal victory for her. Ideally, your milestones and victories should also be a blend of external and internal events. Your road to Next may be long or short; it may have plenty of obvious external markers of success or relatively few. Either way, being able to recognize, acknowledge, and savor your personal victories is a sign that you know who you are and appreciate what's important to you. That is the foundation of self-love.

» Don't Be Afraid to Celebrate

Now that you have these broken out you want to be sure to acknowledge and actually celebrate each one as they happen. This does not mean you need to have a party at a fancy hotel for each one, only that you are conscious of these victories—again, especially the internal ones—and acknowledge them in some way. Celebrating a victory can be as simple as a word of encouragement that you say to yourself or it can be something more easily seen by the outside world. This is for you to decide.

When I worked with Jane, I encouraged her to take the time at each victory to do something to acknowledge and celebrate her success. Having this concrete plan helped to keep her feet on her path and increased her awareness of her victories along the way. Acknowledging and celebrating these victories helped Jane to appreciate herself and recognize the progress she was making.

It does not matter how structured or unstructured you want to be in this process. What matters is that you recognize and take pride in the victories that you establish on your journey. The path to what's next for you will not be straight. It's not for anyone. Your process and goals will shift, but if you know how to shift with them, you will get there. Using these techniques to embrace and celebrate yourself will put you on the path toward loving yourself and merging with the hero inside of you.

Loving yourself is a transformative experience. Once you do it you will no longer be restrained by your inner critic. Instead you will become one with the optimistic part of you, the part that has faith in you. That faith will essential to help you stay the course. Self-doubt is not hard to come by so there's no need to ask for more of it. By reminding yourself of your forward progress on your journey, you will be able to hold some of the armies of your inner critic at bay and reconnect with the hero inside of you.

THE TAKEAWAY

1 You learned about the need for self-love in order to merge with the hero inside of you.

2 You learned about the vast difference between self-love and narcissism and how they relate to confidence and arrogance.

3 You discovered that you were a born optimist.

4 You considered how love was expressed in your family of origin.

5 You learned strategies for how to begin to love yourself, including embracing your "imperfections" and marking and celebrating your victories.

LIVE IN THE NOW

Chapter

10

When we began our journey together you were running in place. Since that time you have opened yourself up to a new vision. You have discovered your purpose, taken action, embraced your process, and reclaimed your true, heroic self.

In this chapter we are going to help you sustain your positive momentum and enhance the New You by combining the New You with the Now You. To do this, we will need to change our focus from the horizon you have created toward the ground beneath your feet. As you do this, you will discover that the real secret to getting to your next big thing has nothing to do with Next: It is about living in the Now.

LIVING IN THE NOW »

You may have heard the phrase "living in the Now" before and dismissed it as too trite, foreign, or granola-y for you. And perhaps it was. But before you decide to skip this section, please give Now a chance. I also ask that you let me explain what living in the Now means, why it's important, and then, specifically, how to integrate it into your life. Until you know these things, you certainly aren't going to want to try to live in the Now—plus you won't know how to do it. We are going to address all of these points so that by the time you reach the end of this chapter you will feel the same way you will when you finish reading this sentence for the second time: focused, present, here, and now.

"Living in the Now" is kind of an odd idea, isn't it? I mean how can you possibly not be living in the Now? If you are alive and reading this, when else could you be living? The turn of the century? The Renaissance?

Living in the Now is a deceptively simple idea. It means that wherever you are physically, you are also there psychologically and emotionally. Where you exist in body, you do so in mind and spirit—wholly, truly, fully—with every ounce of your being. Living in the Now does not necessarily mean that you are happy or joyful. It's just that whatever you are experiencing at that time you are *actually* experiencing it, rather than avoiding it. When you are living in the Now you are consumed—taken, by the present. We talked a bit about this way back in Chapter 2, when we explored your Activities of Joy. When you are so deeply engaged in something because it brings you joy, time is irrelevant— nothing else matters except what you are doing. Living in the Now is a state of emotional and psychological presence that aligns with your physical space, and it is imperative for living an emotionally healthy life. Somewhat ironically, it is also critical for getting to your next big thing.

Before I get too Zen on you—unless you think I already have—let's break this down and see how much of your time you have been spending in the Now. Take the following quiz to find out:

Quiz:

DO YOU LIVE IN THE NOW?

❶ During the past week, how much time have you spent fully present living in the Now?

① Most of the time. You move in and out of it at points, but generally speaking you are living in the Now.

② Some of the time. You have brief flashes of living in the Now, but most of the time you find that you're partially focused elsewhere.

③ Virtually none. You are constantly distracted, anchored to the past, nervously anticipating the future, or otherwise psychologically absent from the Now.

❷ During the past week, how many times have you been so immersed in an activity that when it ended you were surprised at how quickly time had passed?

① You have felt that way at least five times.

② You have felt that way at least once but less than five times.

③ You have not felt that way at all during the past week.

3 Right now, as you read this, how focused are you on these words?

1. 100 percent. You're here. I had you at "right now."
2. At least 70 percent. You're reading this but there is a part of you that is thinking about other things you should be doing.
3. You are rereading this passage for the second or third time because you were distracted.

Let's see how you did. Add up the scores (1, 2, or 3) on the three questions from this quiz and look below to consider where you are now.

✦ ✦

Do You Live in the Now?—Add It Up!

Total Score 3–4: You are living in the Now. Good for you! Don't let me distract you from your smooth, Buddha-like flow—not that I could, of course.

Total Score 5–7: You have moments of being in the Now, but the majority of your time is spent in various states of absence. Keep reading for some suggestions on how to reverse this trend.

Total Score 8–9: Bueller? Bueller? Bueller . . . ? Hello! Hello! (snap, snap) Over here! You are absent. We are going to work on that together.

✦ ✦

If you haven't been living in the Now, let's try to understand where you have been going and why you have been going there.

The reason that you haven't been living in the Now is that in all likelihood you haven't seen the need for it. In fact, you've probably seen the need for *not* living in the Now. As we grow up, and unfortunately, even when many of us are children, we have so many demands placed on our time and energy and so many options for distraction that many of us spend our days either drawn to the future, anchored to the past, or just elsewhere, essentially absent from the present. What does being absent actually mean?

ABSENCE »

When your body is in one place but your mind is somewhere else, you are absent. You can be absent in three different ways. You can escape the Now by going to:

- The Past—by compulsively rehashing events that have already happened
- The Future—by compulsively "spinning" about events that have not yet taken place
- The Elsewhere—by intentionally or unintentionally thinking about events other than those occurring around you or within you, or by using external distractions or substances in order to exit the present

Consider the following quiz to see how much of your time you have been spending in a state of absence:

Quiz:

ARE YOU ABSENT?

❶ During the past week how much time have you spent focused on events from the past?

① None or very little. You have spent the majority of your time living in the Now.

② Some. On more than two or three occasions you found your thoughts unintentionally drifting back to things that have already happened.

③ Practically all. Most of your waking hours have been spent in a state of mind anchored to events from the past.

② **During the past week how much time have you spent focused on events in the future?**

① None or very little. You have spent the majority of your time living in the Now.

② Some. On more than two or three occasions you found your thoughts pulled toward events that had not yet happened.

③ Practically all. Most of your waking hours have been spent in a state of mind where you've been compulsively spinning about things that have not yet come to pass.

③ **How much of the past week have you spent in an *unintentional* state of absence, one in which you weren't deliberately choosing to exit the Now but your mind drifted elsewhere?**

① None or very little. You have spent the majority of your time living in the Now.

② Some. On more than two or three occasions you found your thoughts pulled toward something that was not relevant to where you were.

③ Practically all. Most of your waking hours during the past week have been spent in an unintentional state of distraction.

④ **How many times during the past week have you been in an *intentional* state of absence, either through alcohol or drugs or other distracters?**

① None or very little. You have spent the majority of your time living in the Now.

② Some. On more than two or three occasions you deliberately chose to escape the present by using distracters.

③ Practically all. Most of your waking hours during the past week have been spent in a deliberate state of absence.

Let's see how you did. Add up the scores (1, 2, or 3) on the three questions from this quiz and look below to consider how absent you have been during the past week.

✛ ✛

Are You Absent?—Add It Up!

Total Score 4–6: Not at all. You are here now.

Total Score 7–9: Somewhat. You spend a sizeable portion of your time in a state of distraction or absence. Keep reading for some suggestions on how to be more present.

Total Score 10–12: You are mostly absent. We are going to work on that together.

✛ ✛

Regardless of how absent or present you are in your daily life, you may be wondering Capital S, Capital W: "So What?" So What if I'm absent for most of my life? I thought this book was about what's next, not what's now. I want my money back! Get me the President!

If that's where you're coming from, chill. Let me explain.

What's now is not just important but *imperative* for getting to what's next. Inhabiting a mind-set that is anchored to negative experiences of the past, anxious about the future, or in the elsewhere cheats you out of your own life. If you are not present in your own life, you can't possibly get to what's next for you. Being absent siphons off your most vital energy and removes your presence from the present. When you are held back by the past or *unintentionally* drawn into the unknowable future, it is impossible to live a life infused with joy and meaning.

If you are constantly outside of the Now you will ultimately get stuck and end up running in place. In order to be actively pursuing what's next for you, you will need all of you—the playful you, the purposeful you, and the working you—in order to get there. These parts of you can be hard to come by if you are absent.

» Why Are You Absent?

If having all of you present ultimately enhances your well-being and is essential for getting to your next stage, you may be asking yourself, "Why do I bother escaping the present?" The answer to this question is a simple four-letter word: pain. We are all, thankfully, wired so that when we experience pain we instinctively and instantly move away from it.

Of course, this works for physical pain. When your finger touches something intensely hot you immediately move your hand away without even thinking about it. This also holds true for psychological pain. When we experience psychological discomfort or pain we instinctively try to escape it. The problem is that we can't escape from pain that is inside of us because there is nowhere else to go. Instead we try to do the next best thing: we exit the present. We become absent.

THE THREE ROADS OF ABSENCE: PAST, FUTURE, AND ELSEWHERE »

Leaving the present comes in three forms: Past, Future, and Elsewhere. Let's look at each of these in turn to get a better understanding of your pattern of absence.

» The Past

People who are psychologically anchored to the past tend to be melancholy or depressed. They generally spend their mental energy feeling tethered to what was, rather than what is. The three forms of psychological past dwelling are:

1. Trying to mentally "undo" events that have already happened
2. Ruminating over sad experiences
3. Pining for the "good old days" and wishing they would return

The tragic nature of melancholy thoughts is that we are driven by the wish to go back to the past in order to feel better in the present. We feel compelled by this because we are naturally drawn to deal with dilemmas and will persist in an effort to arrive at a solution to even insoluble problems. However, trying to undo, redo, or relive the past is impossible and just leads to feeling powerless in the present.

Consider how the insidious nature of depressive thoughts impacted a former patient of mine.

Dana

Dana was a twenty-nine-year-old teacher who had been in a long-term relationship. We were working on some career-related issues, and in general I found her to be a sunny, optimistic woman who spent most of her time living in the Now. We had been working together for several months when her long-time boyfriend broke up with her. She stopped going to work, stopped eating, and slept constantly. Dana only came to my office sporadically. When she did, she spent most of her energy remembering the good times with her ex-boyfriend, trying to figure out what she did wrong, and imagining different choices she could have made that would have prevented him from breaking up with her. Dana was romanticizing her ex-boyfriend, yet before he had broken up with her she had expressed serious doubts about him and reservations about their relationship.

She had become psychologically tethered to the past. The present and centered woman whom I had come to know was gone. It took some time and work for the shock to wear off and for Dana to regain her present-day focus and ability to live in the Now. She ultimately did it, but for several months she was running from her present pain by un-doing, ruminating, and pining for an imaginary past.

Is there anything in Dana's experience that sounds familiar to you? Perhaps you have had a similar experience in which you felt trapped by your past.

When you have had a negative, or even a traumatic experience, it is not uncommon to spend some time psychologically inhabiting the past. Yet this way of thinking can take over your mind and prevent you from moving on and getting to what's next for you. We are going to change that by getting you back to living in the Now. Before we get there, let's look at two other ways of escaping the present: jumping to the future and going elsewhere.

›› The Future

Anxiety works in a very similar way to depression. The difference is that the psychological process takes place in the future instead of the past. People who are anxious are fearful of what's next. In an attempt to reduce their fears, such people exit the Now and enter an imaginary, distorted future.

They try to escape the present moment but get caught in an endless loop by attempting to work through a situation that is not here yet.

This is the seductive, insidious nature of anxiety. When you are fearful of the unknown future and, your mind tricks you into thinking that you are preparing by running through every possible scenario that you can imagine. However, you don't have the true facts or realities of these experiences that concern you because *they are not here yet, and they may never be*. Every attempt you make to solve the problem fuels the feeling of discomfort and uncertainty because on a subconscious level you appreciate that the future is unknowable—and yet you are trying desperately to know it. You work and rework a math problem when you don't have all of the numbers. Not surprisingly, you become stymied and frustrated time and again, since any solution that you have derived is, by definition, wrong because it lacks all of the variables, including the most important one: *being in the actual situation*; living in the Now.

As an example of how anxiety does its dirty deed, consider the experience of a former patient of mine named Lance.

Lance

Lance had been married for two and a half years, and he and his wife were considering having children. His wife, who found me through a friend of hers, encouraged Lance to meet with me because he was extremely anxious about the prospect of becoming a father.

Shortly after coming in, Lance told me that on the one hand he wanted to be a dad, but whenever he thought about it he became nervous. When I asked him to tell me what he thought about when he felt this way, at first he couldn't say. A little bit later in the session Lance told me he was worried that his wife would not let him sleep until the afternoon on Sundays once he became a dad.

Lance worked an extremely demanding job, putting in brutally long hours, and he partied hard on the weekends in order to blow off steam. On Saturday nights he would often drink to the point that he was hung over on Sunday morning and needed to sleep late to recover. He told me that he desperately needed that time or his work week would be shot.

Lance's anxiety clearly had to do with more than just sleeping in on Sunday mornings, but it underscored the nature of anticipatory anxiety: Lance had become gripped by concerns that didn't exist because he imagined his current self in a future scenario—a logical impossibility.

He was trying to envision the present "Hard-core partying Lance" as the future "Father Lance," and he couldn't figure out how to reconcile the two images in his mind. Lance anticipated that after he had a child he would continue with his current cycle of burning the candle at both ends—working eighty-plus-hour weeks and going out drinking hard on Saturday nights, while also caring for a child. This couldn't exist, and he knew it, and the disconnect fueled his anxiety. Incidentally, even though I stopped working with Lance, he has since checked in with me and, sure enough, his partying has slowed down considerably and he is a happy, hard-working dad who still lets loose from time to time—just not every weekend.

- -

What about you? Do you ever unintentionally leave the present and inhabit a future that doesn't yet exist in an attempt to feel more in control? Is there anything in Lance's story that reminds you of your own experience? Before we learn how to lead you from the clutches of anxiety, let's look at the final way of leaving the Now: Going elsewhere.

›› Elsewhere

What does it mean to go "Elsewhere?" and what exactly is wrong with it?

Actually, there is nothing wrong with going elsewhere as long as you *choose* to go there. Everyone goes elsewhere from time to time by thinking of people, places, or things not directly relevant to the present moment or by "tuning out" in different ways including: watching mindless television or movies, consuming other media, drinking alcohol, or using drugs. Most people go elsewhere during frightening, unpleasant, or boring situations. In fact, mentally exiting the moment makes good sense in some cases, especially if it is during an overwhelming situation.

For all three forms of escape—Past, Future, or Elsewhere—the key considerations are intention and choice. When I refer to compulsively rehashing events of the past or spinning about events that have not yet taken place, I want to emphasize that I am not talking about the deliberate decision to think about the past with the goal of learning from it or choosing to focus on the future with the intention of planning for it. And when I make reference to escaping to elsewhere, remember: we all do this by choice from time to time. The problem of absence is when it is *not* a choice or when we choose to do it so often that the temporary escape becomes permanent avoidance.

I hope that these distinctions are helpful to you and speak to ways that you may have escaped or tried to escape from the Now. If one or more of these forms of absence feels like you, it may be worth taking a moment to understand more specifically how you tend to try to exit the Now and to learn where it is that you go when you escape.

Exercise:

HOW DO YOU LEAVE AND WHERE DO YOU GO?

Take out your journal or a piece of paper. Make three columns labeled: Past, Future, and Elsewhere.

Think back over the past day and about times you *unintentionally* escaped the Now by going to the past, future, or elsewhere.

Write down these experiences in the appropriate column on the paper in front of you. Make some notes about where your mind went.

Do you see any consistencies or patterns? Are you more often drawn to the past, the future, or elsewhere? Have you been using certain repeating patterns of escape over and over again? Are you using television? Alcohol? Fantasy?

Here's an example of how this might look:

PAST	FUTURE	ELSEWHERE
Thinking about David. Missing him. Wishing he was still with me. Feeling guilty about not giving him the picture. David was the best man I ever knew. There won't ever be anyone as generous and fun as him.	A little worried about never finding another man like David.	

This person is clearly struggling with a loss, and all of her thoughts relate to David in one way or another, but most of her absence is tied to the past rather than the future or elsewhere. What about you? When you are absent, where do you tend to go?

THREE STRATEGIES FOR LIVING IN THE NOW: HONOR, PRESENCE, AND MEDITATION »

Are there certain intrusive thoughts that keep dragging you back to the past, pushing you toward the future, or pulling you elsewhere? Are these thoughts getting in the way of your living in the Now? If so, let's deal with them now.

» Honor

If you noticed any consistent patterns of thought on your list, that means that your mind is trying to tell you something and isn't going to take no for an answer. Don't even bother trying to ignore those thoughts or feelings, because, well, you can't. It is possible to force them out of your mind for a time, but it is not so easy to do and the mere effort of trying to force a thought out of your head takes up a substantial amount of mental energy. Plus, they will be back before you know it. Instead of fighting yourself and the thoughts that are circling around your mind, you are going to learn to honor them.

I recommend a three-step approach to honoring thoughts or feelings that are getting in the way of your living in the Now:

1. *Listen* to your thoughts for a moment or two. Stop what you are doing and ask yourself, "What are these thoughts about?" Sometimes even speaking the thoughts out loud or writing them down helps you to hear what your mind or heart is telling you. If you do decide to write the thoughts out, keep them brief. Remember, the goal is to show deference to your thoughts and feelings so that you can clear your mental desktop in order to get you back to living in the Now.

2. *Acknowledge* the importance of these thoughts or feelings. Remember, you can't beat 'em, so join 'em. Your intrusive thoughts will no longer need to scream at you to get your attention if you work with them. If these thoughts keep coming up and are getting in the way of the Now, they must be useful to you in some way. You

can effectively turn down the volume on your intrusive thoughts by recognizing them as important and worthy of your time and attention—just not the *present* time and your *current* attention. If you consciously acknowledge the value of them, your intrusive thoughts should settle down. By actually stating (either silently or out loud, depending on your circumstances) that these thoughts have merit and will be addressed, you may be able to mute them, at least temporarily. Now it's time to commit to giving these thoughts their due.

3. *Commit* the time, energy, and resources to addressing these thoughts or feelings. Picking a time and putting it down in your journal, phone, appointment planner, or desktop calendar will likely help you in this process. You may also put in writing a commitment to engage with these thoughts at another time, but if you do write down your commitment to your intrusive thoughts, again please keep it brief.

Now here's the kicker: You *must* keep this commitment. If you listen to and acknowledge the value of these thoughts and then commit the resources to addressing your intrusive thoughts but don't actually follow up on your commitment, it may be harder to quiet your thoughts next time. If you do write down your commitment, you may want to then start and end your writing with a positive affirmation that you are using this time to be present.

Consider how this worked for my patient Peter, the writer, whom I mentioned in Chapter 8.

Peter

Peter found that he was continually distracted by thoughts of his stepfather while he was trying to write his novel. He said that after he cleared the decks to write, he suddenly felt the urgent need to do something about his stepfather's health problems (which were significant but not emergent). He decided to honor his thoughts and feelings about his stepfather as well as his work as a writer. He wrote down the following: "I am writing down my intrusive thoughts about Carl so I can continue writing today. I am concerned about his health and need to take an active role in consulting with his docs. I will call mom and Carl tomorrow morning at 8:30 to set up an appointment with his doctor, but for the next 75 minutes I am working on Section Two [of my book.]" That was all it took to allow him to come back to the present and to continue writing that day.

- -

Honoring thoughts that are drawing you out of the Now can be helpful on multiple levels: It acknowledges the importance of these unprocessed thoughts and feelings, it helps you to temporarily clear your head, and it clarifies what you are doing now. By going through this three-step process of listening, acknowledging, and committing future resources to these intrusive thoughts, you are most likely to render them inert for the time being. Then you'll be able to get down to living in the Now and getting on to what's next.

›› Presence

One of the keys to being where you are is . . . being where you are. We often spend so much of our waking lives in a state of distraction that we don't take the time to fully take in what is around us. If you are finding yourself pulled away from the Now, try the following exercise:

Exercise:

WHERE ARE YOU NOW?

Look around you—all around you. Take in what you see with your eyes. Write down (or if you don't have a pen, you can say it out loud) what you see. Bring your focus in to your immediate surroundings and for one minute try to think only of what's around you. Any thoughts or words that you say or write that have anything to do with things not around you don't count. If you slip up, try it again. This is a way of training your mind to be in the Now. Once you are grounded in the present, you can choose what you want to think about or work on.

Incidentally, I have used a variation of this exercise when I have advised couples who are arguing. Many times couples' arguments start out based in the moment but quickly spiral out of the present and pull in past events or future concerns. If you find that this is happening to you, try spending a few minutes with your partner only talking about what you can see around you. It can be a bit hard, but it's also kind of fun. Plus, it will cut down on your fighting.

Okay, I've saved the best strategy for getting you back to the Now for last: meditation. Here it goes:

» Meditation

If these other strategies are not working and you are feeling carried away by rogue thoughts or emotions, you can try to bring yourself home to the Now by using another strategy that will, at the very least, momentarily disrupt your intrusive thoughts or psychological displacement into the past, future, or elsewhere. By focusing your energy on your five senses you can ground yourself in the Now. This exercise can have a centering effect and is a type of brief meditation. There are countless ways to do it. One that has worked well for some of my patients involves focusing on *only* what can be perceived in the present through the five senses, one sense at a time. This progression can be effective in breaking free from distraction. As you read through the next few paragraphs, I recommend that you try to do the exercise one sense at a time with the book in hand. Then try it again without the book.

The Five Senses

The exercise starts with your sense of smell (the olfactory sense). The reason for this is that smell is the only one of the sensory systems that goes from the sensory organ (the nose) directly to where it is processed in the brain. The messages from all the other senses (sight, hearing, touch, and taste) are sent to a "relay station," in the brain (the thalamus) before they travel to other parts of the brain where the messages are received. Your sense of smell goes directly to the place in your brain that processes memories and basic emotions, which is why particular smells can quickly trigger memories from long ago and have a powerful influence on your emotions. Even the faintest smell of a roast as you pass by a neighbor's house can immediately draw you back to the Christmas you spent at your grandmother's house when you were four years old. Smell is an incredibly powerful sense.

If you sniff around for the smells in your environment, your mind will try to connect what you smell with what you know or how you feel. It will instantly draw you away from intrusive thoughts. Once you have removed yourself from the distracting thoughts, you can use your other four senses to bring yourself back to the present.

Exercise:

BACK TO THE PRESENT

Using what you now know about being in the present, try the following guided meditation. Read through the exercise first and then try doing it on your own. I'll meet you in the present when you're done!

- Say the word, "Smell." Focus all of your mental energy on your sense of smell. What do you smell right now? Coffee? Paint? Candles? Lunch? Shampoo? If you're not sure, keep on sniffin'. You will be drawn to the present.
- Say the word, "Hear." Draw your energy away from your olfactory sense and toward your auditory sense. What do you hear right now? What is making those sounds? Are they near or far? Try to bring your focus to the sounds that you may not have been conscious of until just this second: the faint hum of a refrigerator motor, the din of the cars outside, or the almost imperceptible buzz of a fluorescent bulb. Directing your attention toward the less dramatic sounds in your environment can draw you into the present if you focus on them. When you are focused elsewhere, these types of sounds naturally fade into the background. Turn up the volume and your mind will meet you in the moment.
- Say the word, "Taste." What tastes remain in your mouth? Can you still perceive the tartness of the orange juice that you drank an hour ago, or the minty flavor of the tartar control toothpaste that you used to brush? What about the faint taste of lasagna that you ate before you sat down to read? Can you still perceive the mild pulsing of your tongue from where

you tasted the bitterness of the coffee a few moments ago? Focusing on the experience of taste requires you to shut out your other senses if you are trying to analyze what you taste in the present but may not have been conscious of until the current time.

- Say the word, "Touch." Draw your attention to the other parts of your body. What physical sensations are you experiencing now? Is your body touching anything as you read this? Are you seated? If so, can you feel the weight of the backs of your legs against the chair? Is your back pressed in against your couch? Are your legs crossed? Are your feet up on a table? Do you feel the heaviness of your heel bone on the floor? If you are standing, do you sense the weight of your body resting on your hips, quads, and feet? Are you leaning on a pole? How does it feel? Cold? Hard? Do you feel the pressure of your elbows on the table in front of you? Are you leaning on the table or wall? How does the contact feel? This is where your body is at this instant.
- Say the word, "See." Now you are looking at the words on this page, but when you look up, what will you see? What is around you? A blank canvas? A piece of paper? What else is in your field of vision? Your hand? The couch? A table? A train platform? Your sleeves? Take it in. This is where you are now.

If you try this approach and it doesn't work perfectly for you, try tailoring it to your needs. This exercise has worked with many, though not all, of my patients. Some patients have said that they like this meditation because they can do it anywhere. Others have said that it feels somewhat uncomfortable, which is fine. The goal is to break with distraction. As with all of the exercises in this book, do what works for you.

There are many other types of meditations, such as mantra meditation (in which you say a word or phrase over and over again), or focus meditation (in which you focus all of your energy on a single object), to help draw you into the present. The present is where you want to be in order to get to Next.

THE TAKEAWAY

In this chapter you learned about the importance of living in the Now for getting to what's next.

You learned that living in the Now means that wherever you are physically, you are also there psychologically and emotionally.

You discovered the three different paths of absence: being tied to the past, pulled into the future, or dragged elsewhere.

You concentrated on your own patterns of absence and learned three strategies to bring you back to the present, which involved honoring your intrusive thoughts, taking stock of your current surroundings, and meditating on your five senses.

SHARE
YOURSELF

Chapter

As you now know, getting to your next big thing is not just about getting you from running in place to moving with purpose. It is a story without an ending. It is your story—your journey that you will make and renew time and again throughout your life. You have already traveled far. The ultimate part of your passage involves connecting you with other people through the act of sharing yourself. If you are wondering what sharing has to do with getting to what's next, the answer is this: Everything.

Sharing your resources—what you know, what you have experienced, what you feel—with other people is the revelation of your next big thing. Giving is the ultimate sign that you are where you need to be. It is the culmination of knowing yourself, discovering your purpose, embracing your process, and living in the Now. Generosity is a gesture of confidence and faith. People who feel full and present don't just *want* to give—they *need* to give. In contrast, people who feel empty and absent cannot give because they are afraid that they *do not* and *will not* have enough.

You are present. You are moving. You are confident.

It is time to share.

Sharing yourself works on literal and symbolic levels. It is both an act of kindness and a sign of how much you are growing and changing. It is the essence—the key—the secret to reaping the harvest of a life filled with play, purpose, and work. When you give, you receive.

Sharing is the final step on your journey. Let's take it together.

Before we get into the nuts and bolts of why and how to share (and how not to share), let's pause for a moment to check in and see where you are so you can understand how sharing fits in with your process and progress. Take the following quiz to find out:

WHERE ARE YOU NOW?

❶ As you look down at these words, how do you feel compared to when you started the journey to your next big thing?

① You feel that you're reasonably far down the road.

② You feel that you're a little further along than when you first started but you have a ways to go.

③ You feel that you're still running in circles or you have slipped backward.

❷ Right now, in this moment, which of the following statements most closely represents how you feel about yourself?

① You love yourself—scrapes, scars, and scabs—through and through.

② You have learned to appreciate yourself, but you wouldn't say that you fully love yourself just yet.

③ When you started reading this book you felt badly about yourself and it hasn't changed in the slightest. Perhaps it has even gotten worse.

❸ How are you feeling about the process of getting to what's next for you?

① Easy. You know that it is a process and you are comfortable moving and shifting with the ever-changing ground beneath your feet.

② Okay. You have vision and purpose but you're still struggling with your inner critic. At times you find it hard to take action, be present, and love yourself.

③ Lost or spiraling down. You haven't been able to make use of any of the exercises or suggestions in this book.

Let's see how you did. Add up the scores (1, 2, or 3) on the three questions from this quiz and look below to consider where you are at this point in your journey.

Where Are You Now?—Add It Up!

Total Score 3–4: You are at Next.

Total Score 5–7: You are well on your way.

Total Score 8–9: You are still running in place or slipping backward.

Regardless of exactly where you are on your journey, it is time to share. Look below at the section that relates to where you are (At Next, On Your Way, or Running in Place/Slipping Back) to discover why you should share now.

›› At Next

If you are already at Next, you are feeling strong, active, present, and full. You have vanquished your inner critic and released your inner hero. You have faith in your vision and purpose. Now it's time to give back. Sharing is the natural extension of the fullness you feel because you know the truth: the more there is, the more there is (no, that's not a typo.)

›› On Your Way

If you are in the second category, On Your Way, you are active and moving but you may be struggling from time to time. Sharing yourself with the world around you can help push you further along your path.

Remember the flight attendant analogy from Chapter 9? Flight attendants instruct the passengers who are traveling with small children to put their oxygen masks on first so that they will be more capable of helping their children with their masks. The idea behind the instruction is that if parents try to put their kids' masks on first, both the parents and children are at greater risk. If you are on your way, you are no longer struggling for breath, so you can, and should, use your good fortune to help others get oxygen. Even if you don't always feel strong, you are. Show your strength; grow your strength by giving it away. The act of giving makes you stronger and pushes you further. Sharing without fear can make you fearless. For you, sharing is a symbol of how far you've come and a catalyst to go further.

» Running in Place or Slipping Back

If you are Running in Place or Slipping Back, this is going to shock you—but you too should share yourself with others. Why? I can think of three reasons, and I'm not even trying that hard:

- First, donating a part of yourself forges a connection between you and those around you. It creates positive energy—the type of energy that helps get you unstuck and moving forward in your life.
- Second, giving of yourself will set an example for other people who will appreciate your generous and noble gesture. Their picture of you can become an inspiration for a new vision of yourself. When others see you as larger than yourself you will begin to do so too, and a positive cycle has begun.
- Finally, sharing yourself with others is charity—and charity is an absolute good. You can give charity for noble reasons or less lofty aims, but it doesn't really matter. Charity is good. Period. Full stop. It doesn't matter why you do it, it only matters *that* you do it. The person who receives your offering is elevated regardless of why you decided to give. The needy don't care that the reason they have food to eat is that you needed a tax break, nor does it matter to the infirm that they are getting medical treatment because you wanted to impress people with your largesse. The fact is they are benefiting from your actions, so your actions are good.

SHARING YOUR JOURNEY »

Everyone has a road to travel. Now that you recognize and are walking your road, you will undoubtedly begin to appreciate how your journey binds you to the other souls who have walked before you, will walk after you, and of course, are walking in time with you. Everyone is connected by the same fundamental struggle. Sharing yourself with others strengthens the invisible bond between you and other people.

Other people—and animals and plants, for that matter—have shared with you. They have contributed and sacrificed for you. Everyone has different experiences of care, some more appropriate and fulfilling than others. Humans are born too weak to survive without the vigilance and support of an adult. When you feel good about and grateful for the care you have received, you will naturally want to share with others in order to replenish the world.

In contrast, if you feel that you have not received enough care, you have even more reason to share. If you have been wronged or mistreated, sharing takes on a greater significance for you. Through the process of contributing to others, you can fill the void created by those who should have provided more for you. By giving of yourself you allow the wounds of the past to heal. The opposite approach, in which you withhold your essence from the world, on principle or in protest, perpetuates negative cycles of resentment and anger. This does nothing to hasten your healing and will ultimately hamper your development.

HOW DO YOU SHARE YOURSELF? »

Now that you are convinced that you need to share yourself, you may be wondering how to do it. In order to share you need to know three things:

1. What you will be sharing
2. Why you are sharing
3. With whom you will be sharing

What you will be sharing are your "resources." Why you will be sharing will depend on the "needs" you see and the people who will receive your giving are your "beneficiaries." We will look at each of these in turn so you can decide how you can best share with others.

» Resources

Regardless of whether your journey has been largely about career development, exploring new relationships, or emotional or spiritual growth, you have gained from walking your path. Your life is expanded and expanding. You have learned things about yourself that you did not know before, you have reclaimed your heroic birthright, you have imagined, you have unearthed your purpose, and you have taken action. You have discovered resources that you never knew you had. Your resources may be internal or external. Internal resources are qualities that only you can see. They include things like faith, discipline, fortitude, action, and drive.

External resources are things that you may have in your life that other people can see. This includes things like money, a new relationship, job, career, or an Activity of Joy. Let's try to figure out what resources you have by using the following exercise:

Exercise:

WHAT ARE YOUR RESOURCES?

Take out your journal or a piece of paper and create two columns. Make the right-hand column about twice as wide as the left-hand column. Label the left-hand column "Resources," and the right-hand column, "Beneficiaries and Needs." In the left column make a list of at least five resources that you currently possess. You may want to categorize them into internal and external resources, but it is not necessary to do so. If you choose to do this just put the word "Internal" or "External" next to your resource.

Here is an example of how this might look:

RESOURCES	BENEFICIARIES AND NEEDS
Faith (Internal)	
Optimism (Internal)	
Empathy (Internal)	
Great boyfriend (External)	
Professional contacts (External)	
Money (External)	

Now that you know what your resources are (what you have to share), let's learn about what's around you to see where your resources meet the needs of other people.

» Beneficiaries and Needs

The key to sharing is matching what you have to share with people who need those resources. Of course, everyone has needs, but everyone's needs are different. In order to find an appropriate match, you will want to do a mental scan of your environment to see if there are any potential beneficiaries whose needs meet your resources. The person or persons you choose to give to don't necessarily need to be people you know. That is entirely up to you. You can always find someone with needs that match your resources; it's just a matter of looking. Some resources are best shared in person while others can be shared over great distances.

Both internal and external resources can be shared with other people. Look over the sample list of resources I gave you for the previous exercise. The list contained six resources: money, professional contacts, faith, optimism, empathy, and a great boyfriend. You probably know how to share money or professional contacts with other people, but what about faith, optimism, or empathy? You might be wondering how, or if, you want to share your great boyfriend with other people, and what exactly that entails.

Allow me to explain.

Faith, optimism, and empathy can be shared with people you know who need those qualities in their lives right now. I'm certain that if you think about it, you can find someone in your world who could use a dose of at least one of those. With regard to "sharing" a great boyfriend, this can require a bit more creativity. One possible way of doing this is to learn about his resources and see if they can be shared with other people in need. The way one of my former patients shared her great boyfriend with a friend of hers was to set up one of his friends with her friend who was looking for a mate. These are ways to share that can make the difference for other people, and for you.

If this is a bit abstract, please consider the following example. This one, unlike the others offered in this book, is from my own life. I feel that it gets at the essence of sharing, which more often than not has nothing to do with money.

Jason

After a few years of working in different hospital jobs, I decided to quit and make a run at starting a private practice. It was very hard at first and, truth be told, I was struggling. I needed to make more money, but I didn't want to go back to my job at Bellevue. I reached out to my friend Jason, an entrepreneur, and asked him for some advice. Instead of advice, he offered me a part-time job in his enterprise while I got my private practice up and running. I don't really know anything about business, but I figured, Why not? I needed the money, I would learn something, and hopefully get to help my friend in the process. At the very least it would be interesting.

The time that I spent working closely with Jason gave me well more than I could have possibly anticipated.

I have known Jason since I was nine years old. He is a true entrepreneur—clever, confident, and bold. During the eighteen months I was employed by his company, I learned a great deal about how the business world works—and also how it doesn't. But one of the most valuable lessons I learned came directly from Jason himself.

My practice was growing, and Jason's company was starting to explode. We were coming to the end of our time working together and we both knew it. Jason and I were in a meeting with some executives at a large, well-respected company when one of the men across the table from us offhandedly called Jason a "risk taker."

Jason asked him, "How am I a risk taker?"

The man responded defensively. "I mean you're an entrepreneur. You are out there—trying things. Either you will succeed or you will fail and that makes you a risk taker."

"I don't see it that way," Jason said. "Between the two of us, I actually think that you are the bigger risk taker."

"How's that? I have a stable job. I work for [a big bank.]"

"Exactly," said Jason. "You work for someone else. If your boss or somebody else makes a mistake, the whole company could go down, which might have nothing to do with you. Your fate may be in someone else's hands. That's pretty risky. As for me, I know myself and if this business doesn't work out, I'll learn from it and start a new one. If that one doesn't work out, I'll learn from it and start again. And I'll keep on going until I succeed. That's not risk. That's faith."

The man across the table stared blankly and the meeting continued. I don't know if he got it. But I did. I'll never forget the words Jason shared, which were exactly the words I needed to hear at that time. They have stayed with me ever since and continue to inspire me on my journey.

- -

Okay, back to you. This is *your* journey. You are here now and are ready to share yourself. You have taken stock of your resources; now we just need to figure out how you are going to share them. Let's start by figuring out what needs you see around you. Try working this out using the exercise below:

Exercise:

BENEFICIARIES AND NEEDS

Take out your journal or a piece of paper and turn back to the chart you made for your resources. We are going to fill in the right-hand side of the chart with the names of people you know (or possibly people you don't know) who might benefit from your resources.

As an example of how this might look, consider the sample chart we used before:

RESOURCES	BENEFICIARIES AND NEEDS
Optimism (Internal)/Faith (Internal)	Sheila—Sheila continues to struggle with her love life. Since I have met Bruce I haven't been hanging out with her much because she is a downer. I should spend more time with her and encourage her to get back out there.
Great boyfriend (External)	Sheila—I know that Bruce doesn't have any single friends to set her up with because I already asked him, but let me see if I can get him to widen his search.

Empathy (Internal)	Ethan—Ethan's sister passed away three weeks ago. I went to the funeral and wake but I haven't reached out to him since then. I should call him this week.
Professional contacts (External)	Jill—She is out of work right now and is starting to feel doubtful about her prospects. I can send an e-mail to anyone who might know anyone who is looking for someone in marketing.
Money (External)	Pam—I know that Pam has been working so hard to get her acting career off the ground. She is struggling and I can't give her money directly because she's too proud, but I can give some money to support her theater company.

Now look at your own list. Where you see matches between potential beneficiaries with needs that match your resources, go to it. Start sharing yourself! You will be glad you did.

What? It's not so easy. Why not? Oh, I see.

Okay, let's address that now.

WHY NOT SHARE YOURSELF? »

Occasionally when I advocate the need for sharing, I have heard patients express reluctance because of a fear that their generosity will be rejected. It is a fair and important question to ask yourself whether you can expect your generosity to be accepted as you intend it to be. In order to increase the chances that you will find a willing beneficiary for your largesse, I suggest going through the following thought process before you decide to share yourself with other people. Ask yourself these two questions:

- Does my potential beneficiary want my resources?
- What is the best way for me to share my resources?

Let's look at each of these questions in turn. Even if you have determined that someone could potentially benefit from your sharing, you might be wrong in one of two important ways:

1. They don't actually need the resource that you want to share.
2. They do need the resource that you want to share but they are not in a place where they can receive it.

These questions can usually be answered by a simple check-in with your potential beneficiary. Basically, in order to determine if you are right, just ask. If the answer to either of these questions is "no," then you either need to find a new potential beneficiary, a new resource to give, or a new way to share it. For example, take a look at the last item on the chart above. The resource listed is "Money" and the beneficiary is "Pam," who "has been working so hard to get her acting career off the ground." However, note that my patient wrote that Pam would not accept money directly because she is too proud.

Rather than force the issue, this person elected to share her resource in an indirect way, by giving money to Pam's theater company. This was a great and clever way around the problem, and Pam did not need to know that her friend gave the money to her company or why she did it.

Remember, when done properly, sharing is an absolute good. It does not need to be done with fanfare or acclaim; it just needs to be done.

When you share yourself you connect with the world. You give back. You replenish the resources and energy that you received. When you have a good experience with sharing yourself, you will find that the world opens up to you in ways that you could not have imagined. Giving yourself over to others is a grand gesture and you will soon see that it works to benefit you and the world around you. The more you share, the more resources there will be for you as well as other people.

If you are unsure about this, start small. What may seem like a very minor share from your point of view can have an outsized impact on the world around you and after you. You never know what even the tiniest gesture can do. Although seeing and experiencing the impact of your share is an incredibly enriching experience, you don't actually need to see it to know it has happened. That is what faith in yourself and your journey is all about.

THE TAKEAWAY

1 In this chapter you took the last step on your journey: Sharing yourself.

2 You came to appreciate that sharing yourself is the culmination of your passage because it works on both literal and symbolic levels.

3 You evaluated where you are on your path and realized that there is value in sharing yourself wherever you are.

4 You considered how you will share by evaluating your resources and comparing them to the needs of those around you.

5 You evaluated whether or not there was a good match between your resources and the needs of potential beneficiaries. If there wasn't, you considered alternative ways of sharing yourself.

MOVING
WITH
PURPOSE

Welcome to Next! You have done it. You are here now.

You are moving—but not just moving: You are moving with purpose. You have come through an incredible journey and you are still traveling. You are on the road toward a fuller life.

When you began this process you were running in place—trapped by habits, behaviors, relationships, or a job. Whatever the source of your problem, it was no longer working for you. Since that time you have come to know yourself. You have learned how to play and imagine a new horizon for you. You have discovered your purpose. You faced your inner critic and lived to tell about it. And through writing your personal Statement of Purpose you have taken concrete steps to define how you will live a life filled with meaning.

You have moved beyond mere planning and taken action toward living the life you want. Along the way you have learned to embrace your process and to learn and grow from each experience. You confronted the three-headed monster of Passivity, Perfectionism, and Procrastination, and re-emerged on the other side. When you did, you released the hero inside of you that was there all along. As your hero began calling the shots and you took bold steps toward Next, you came to appreciate the value of living in the Now and the need to share what you've learned with the world around you. And now you are here, feeling the flow and glow of your inner force. You are powerful yet humble. You are calm, centered, and present. You are generous, giving, and kind. You are flexible and strong—you yield but are not toppled. You are serene, easy, and present. Welcome to Next!

A PLACE TO REST ALONG THE WAY »

As you now know, there is a big difference between knowing your path and walking your path. Knowing your path takes courage; walking it takes faith and action. You have come far, but you may be wandering or wondering where you are. If you had a precise goal in mind—a new job, different and healthier relationships, or a better sense of yourself—the answer about where you are may be clear. On the other hand, if you know that you are moving but you don't yet have the concrete result you wanted, it may be somewhat harder to tell if you have gotten to where you need to be. Even if you haven't achieved the precise goals that you set for yourself, you are in a better and healthier place than when you started walking the walk.

Remember, the journey to Next is just that: a journey. There is no final destination, just resting points along the way where you check in and look around in order to savor where you are and see what else you want to do.

This chapter is one of those resting points. We are going to take some time to check in to see how far you've come and where you might want to focus your energies next. Some parts of this chapter may seem like they are just a review of where you've been; if you are feeling better and unstuck you may be tempted to skip it, but I would suggest you go through the quizzes and exercises here so you can carry forth what you have learned along the way to your next adventure.

Take the following quiz to see how far you've come:

Quiz:

CHECKING IN

❶ **How have you been spending the bulk of your time during the past week?**

① You have spent most of your time engaged in meaningful work, joyful play, and focused purpose.

② You have been actively pushing toward what's next for you.

③ You have been mostly running in place.

❷ **Think about your three closest relationships now. Which of the following best describes how you feel about them?**

① You feel that they are a source of pride, strength, and inspiration.

② You feel that they are a source of mild comfort to you, but not much else.

③ Your closest relationships are a tremendous source of stress or distress.

③ During the past week or so, how much time have you been spending using your mind to play with new ideas and imagine new horizons?

① A lot more than you used to and it's making a big difference for how you're approaching your future.

② A little bit. You haven't been actively trying to spend chunks of time playing or imagining a new future, but you feel more open to using these tools to get you pushing forward.

③ None. You don't see how these tools can help you.

④ Which of these three statements best describes how you are feeling about yourself?

① You have been moving toward what's next for you with determination and faith. Very little has been getting in your way.

② You have had moments of vision and action and determination toward getting to what's next for you, but also moments of significant struggle with your inner critic calling the shots.

③ You can't seem to get any traction on your vision or taking action on your next big thing.

⑤ Over the past two weeks or so, when you have felt yourself slipping back into old patterns that weren't working for you, how have you responded?

① You haven't been slipping back into old patterns, or on the few occasions when you did you were able to successful apply the strategies and exercises from this book to get back to moving with purpose.

② You have been aware of these digressions and have been trying to get yourself refocused on where you are now and what you want to be doing next. You haven't always been successful, but you have been trying.

③ You have been slipping but you hadn't noticed it until just now.

⑥ When you think about your future, how do you feel?

① Optimistic. You have renewed faith in yourself and abilities.
② Fair. At moments you believe that the future will be better for you, but you still have your doubts.
③ Pessimistic. You just don't see the way forward.

Let's see how you did. Add up the scores (1, 2, or 3) on the six questions from this quiz and look below to consider where you are now.

✚ ✚

Checking In—Add It Up!

Total Score 6–9: You are well on your way to what's next for you. Keep going.

Total Score 10–14: You are moving forward. You may have a few areas that need some more attention as you get to what's next. It may be worth checking out the next exercise, Reviewing the Ten Steps, to see if you can isolate and build on the areas of your journey that need additional attention.

Total Score 15–18: Something is not working for you. In order to figure out what that is, consider trying the next exercise, titled Reviewing the Ten Steps, in order to see what you need to focus on now.

✚ ✚

Checking in with yourself every once in a while allows you to not only see how far you've come and where you are standing, but also to evaluate the road ahead. Sometimes if we are only focused on moving forward it is easy to forget where we have been and, perhaps more importantly, where we are. In fact, I have seen some patients who have come to me in order to help decide and take action on what's next do just that but not even realize what they have done.

As an example, let's return to my patient Tara, whom I mentioned in Chapter 3.

Tara

If you will recall, Tara had originally come to me in crisis just after discovering that her husband had been having an affair with one of his colleagues. As I began my inquiry, I discovered that her once-steady marriage had slowly become uneven and was now teetering on the edge of oblivion. One of the reasons their relationship had come to a breaking point was that she and Ed no longer played together. They stopped imagining a future together. That was the culture that created a break in their trust, in their bond. It was the culture that fostered the distance between them. It was the culture that Ed wanted to leave, not his wife and not his family. When Ed sensed an opportunity to escape he took it. That's when things fell apart.

As Tara opened herself up to playing and imagining during the therapy, she imagined a life that was actually not so dissimilar from the one she had. She considered her values and determined her purpose and found that the life she had been leading was generally in line with what was important to her. There were a few things that needed changing, of course, though somewhat surprisingly, her relationship with Ed was not the first item on her list.

Through the exercises we did, Tara discovered that what she really wanted, and actually needed for herself, was to go back to work. She was good at what she did and had worked hard to build a successful career. Giving that up made sense at the time but her kids were older now and she realized that she missed the sense of accomplishment and purpose that she had felt when she was working. Tara also recognized that by staying home she felt too emotionally vulnerable to Ed. She was no longer able to shrug off his bad moods but instead took them personally. She thought that she had been doing something wrong and retreated from their relationship.

Tara realigned her life with joy and purpose, and through her couples therapy with Ed, they rebuilt their marriage. It was intensely hard at first. Tara was furious with Ed for his infidelity, and for a long time she was uncertain if she could ever trust him again. She ultimately admonished him that she could forgive but she would not forget. Over time she invited him back into their home and they began to resume their life together. Through a lot of painful work they rebuilt the fabric of the trust between them and slowly but surely they began to imagine a future together.

One day Tara came into session, and for the first time ever she really had nothing to say. She asked me what to do next. It seemed that she already knew.

Tara made her decision about what she wanted her path to be and she had been taking action on it all along. She was working again, and so was her relationship with Ed. They were playing and working and she once again felt that her life had purpose. She didn't need to be in therapy anymore. She was exactly where she needed to be. Tara had already taken her next step—until that moment she just hadn't realized it.

- -

» Circling Back to You

How about you? Where are you on your journey? Are you living with play, purpose, and work? Do you still feel stuck in some areas of your life? Are you different from when you began considering your next big thing? Try the exercise below to chart where you are:

Exercise:

REVIEWING THE TEN STEPS

Before you move on to your next adventures, we should take some time to consider if and where you might want to spend some of your energy now. Are there areas along your path that you feel you might want to focus on? Let's consider the ten steps you have taken and see how far you've come along your journey to Next. Answer the questions below and fill in your answers on the following chart:

CHART: WHERE ARE YOU NOW?			
Step	Very well (1)	So-so (2)	Not so well (3)
1. Know Yourself			
2. Imagine Yourself			

3. Discover Your Purpose			
4. Face Your Inner Critic			
5. Take Action			
6. Embrace Your Process			
7. Defeat the Three-Headed Monster			
8. Reclaim Your Inner Hero			
9. Live in the Now			
10. Share Yourself			

» STEP ONE. Know Yourself

How well do you know yourself? Step One involved learning about who you are now by reviewing what you do (roles), what's important to you (values), and what brings you the feeling that what you are doing and what is important to you are aligned (joy). How well do you feel that you know these aspects of yourself?

- Very well. I know my roles, values, and joy like the back of my hand.
- So-so. I have a decent sense of them but I don't feel that I really know them.
- Not so well. I did the exercises in Chapter 2 but I just don't feel that I have a complete understanding of my roles, values, or joys.

» STEP TWO. Imagine Yourself

How well do you feel that you are able to use play and imagination to envision your next steps and get yourself unstuck when you are not sure what to do next?

- Very well. I appreciate how play and imagination help me to picture what's next. I feel comfortable using these tools and don't feel inhibited or afraid of my thoughts.
- So-so. I understand how play and imagination are my natural tools that can help me see a new future, but at times I feel inhibited or afraid to play with ideas or imagine what's next for me.
- Not so well. I don't see the need for imagining or playing with new ideas, either because they seem like they are for children and not serious adults or because I am afraid of what it might be like to let my imagination run wild.

» STEP THREE. Discover Your Purpose

How well do you feel that you are connected to your core values and that they are guiding your actions in order to live a life of purpose?

- Very well. I am in touch with my core values and I am using them as my North Star in order to live a life of purpose.
- So-so. I feel connected to my core values but I don't fully appreciate how they can give my life focus and direction.
- Not so well. I don't feel connected to my values and don't understand how they can serve as a guide for my life.

» STEP FOUR. Face Your Inner Critic

How well do you understand your inner critic? Can you see him as separate from you? How are you doing in your efforts to keep him from impeding your progress toward your next big thing?

- Very well. I know when he's talking to me. I am not always able to channel my inner hero, but I am working hard to face my inner critic when he surfaces.
- So-so. I can see my inner critic as separate from me at times and I do struggle with him, but he seems to overpower me more often than not.
- Not so well. Either I can't seem to separate from him or when I do I immediately go running back to him. He seems to have a very strong hold over me.

» STEP FIVE. Take Action

How well did you get past the initial barriers to taking action on your next big thing?

- Very well. I assessed my bandwidth and the other barriers to starting taking action. I made the time I needed to get started.
- So-so. I was able to work through several barriers to getting started, but it is still a struggle and I am constantly stopping and starting.
- Not so well. I evaluated my bandwidth and decided that I have the space in my life for taking action on what's next, but I can't seem to do it just now.

» STEP SIX. Embrace Your Process

How well are you doing thinking about—and more importantly, treating—what's next as a process that does not have a definitive stopping point but is a continual journey about living a life of joy and meaning?

- Very well. I appreciate that this is a process and I can see obstacles as opportunities that continually help push me forward.
- So-so. At times I can see getting to Next as a process. I struggle between having faith in who I am becoming and living in fear that I will never change.
- Not so well. I see what's next as a single goal and if I don't achieve exactly what I envision I have failed and will never become the person I wish to be.

» STEP SEVEN. Defeat the Three-Headed Monster

Have you been able to push past the Cerberus to claim the life you want? How well have you been able to understand and address your tendencies toward Passivity, Procrastination, and Perfectionism?

- Very well. At times I still experience Passivity, Procrastination, and Perfectionism, but by and large I have found my triggers and am using them to push me past the three-headed monster.
- So-so. I continue to struggle with Passivity, Procrastination, and Perfectionism. Some days they win and some days I win. It's a constant battle for me.
- Not so well. Passivity, Procrastination, and Perfectionism are always with me. I can never seem to get past them.

» STEP EIGHT. Reclaim Your Inner Hero

How well are you able to see and channel the optimistic voice inside of you that wants to imagine a new and exciting future and run toward it with abandon?

- Very well. She is with me most of the time, reminding me of my promise and potential. She helps me mark my milestones and victories.
- So-so. I can see him now and again. I am continually trying to summon him to help me along my path.
- Not so well. My inner hero is still hiding and hasn't been leading me at all since picking up this book.

» STEP NINE. Live in the Now

How well do you feel you are doing with living a fully present life, where your mind and body are inhabiting the same space at the same time?

- Very well. At least half of my waking hours are spent in the Now.
- So-so. I am fully present for less than half of my waking hours, but I get there at times.
- Not so well. I am constantly in a state of absence, anchored to the past, nervously anticipating the future or drawn elsewhere.

» STEP TEN. Share Yourself

How well do you feel you have been doing sharing yourself with those around you?

- Very well. I feel comfortable sharing myself with those near and far and have been actively doing so.
- So-so. I appreciate how important sharing myself with other people is for my journey, but I still struggle with it at times.
- Not so well. I am concerned that by sharing I won't have enough for me, or that my gifts won't be well received by others.

Now look at the answers you filled in on the Where Are You Now? chart. Any areas that you have filled in a "1" for "Very well" or a "2" for "So-so" indicate that you are either past that point in your journey or you are actively making progress in that area. Those are victories to be celebrated with pride. It doesn't matter so much whether you filled in a "1" or a "2," because both of them indicate active engagement and as long as you are moving with purpose and faith, you will get there. Keep it up and you will continue to feel a sense of fullness in those spheres of your life.

Any areas where you filled in a "3" for "Not so well" need a little more focus. Take a look at those areas, but before you do, consider rereading Chapter 5 (Face Your Inner Critic). In all likelihood you have a tough and tenacious inner critic who is getting in your way. Try the exercises in Chapter 5 again to see how you can go face to face with your inner critic and come through his wall of insults and doubt. Your inner critic is the voice of fear inside of you and he can be a bully—but if you look hard enough, you can always find the fear inside of the bully. Keep at it and keep at him, he will fall and your inner hero will rule the day, and your life. Every time you try, you make progress, you will wear him down. Remember: Over time the persistence of water overcomes mountains.

To help clarify this point, let's return to my patient Reggie, whom I mentioned in Chapter 9.

Reggie

If you recall, Reggie was a twenty-seven-year-old man who wanted to publish a novel. He had completed a manuscript but was reluctant to show it to other people out of a fear that they might not like it.

He ultimately showed it to his boss, Andrew, who was well connected in the publishing world. It took Andrew several weeks to get back to Reggie, which he originally thought of as a defeat. However, through our work together he was able to see this as an internal victory over his fear. When Andrew did get back to Reggie, he received Reggie's work extremely well. Andrew was impressed with Reggie's skill as a writer. He suggested that Andrew make one section into a short story that he could submit to a major literary magazine to further his career. They worked on this together, and the piece was published some time later. Having his work praised by Andrew and seeing his work published in a well-regarded magazine helped Reggie along his path and allowed him to continue to develop as a writer.

One of the significant factors that contributed to this victory was Reggie's approach to his process. He was flexible and willing to learn. Had he simply said, "Well, my manuscript is meant to be a novel, not a short story," things might not have progressed as well as they did. Instead, Reggie was able to take in his boss's feedback and extract the lessons from it, and have his story published in a major magazine. Through his approach Reggie was able to transform his "defeat" into a string of internal and external victories that aided him in his journey.

I stopped working with Reggie some time ago, but I know that he is still writing because I have seen his work appear in many places. If writing a novel is still his aspiration, which I suspect it is, he is well on his way to doing it. And I am certain, with every fiber of my being, that he will do it. More importantly, however, I am confident that he is living a meaningful life that is filled with play, purpose, and work.

- -

Now it is your time to do the same. Through these pages we have traveled many roads together—some of them filled with demons and monsters, some with imagination and wonder. What matters is that you have traveled. You have taken action and steps toward embracing, creating, and receiving a life filled with meaning and joy. It is the life you were meant to lead.

The journey that you are on is both unique and universal. Your path has never been walked before. If it had, it wouldn't be your path—it would be someone else's. The journey itself is one that we all make. Everyone walks it. We each must walk it separately, but not alone. You will share your journey with those around you, and through the act of walking it you become interconnected with those who walked before you, those who walk with you, and those who will walk after you. I thank you for allowing me to be part of your journey. As you continue, I encourage you to remember that what you are seeking is both inside and outside of you. If you keep this in your mind and heart, you will be well served when hope feels thin.

There were many ideas in this book. My wish is that at least some of them were, and will be, of assistance to you as you travel on. If you take one thing away from reading this book, please let it be this: You are a miracle.

There has never been another soul like you; nor can there, or will there, ever be. Make the most of the miracle of you by living a life filled with play, purpose, and work. Give of yourself without losing yourself. What you share will come back to you in riches greater than you can imagine.

THE TAKEAWAY

1 You have made it through the wilderness and come through on the other side. You are moving with purpose.

2 In this chapter you checked in with yourself in order to take stock of where you are now.

3 You reviewed the ten steps that we took together on this journey:

Step 1. Know Yourself
Step 2. Imagine Yourself
Step 3. Discover Your Purpose
Step 4. Face Your Inner Critic
Step 5. Take Action
Step 6. Embrace Your Process

Step 7. Defeat the Three-Headed Monster
Step 8. Reclaim Your Inner Hero
Step 9. Live in the Now
Step 10. Share Yourself

4 You evaluated the areas where you want to invest your energy as you continue to move forward in the adventure of life.

5 You learned that you are a miracle. You know that living a life filled with play, purpose, and work will allow you to make the most of the miracle of you.

Absence, 192–200. *See also* Living in
the Now
Are You Absent? quiz, 192–95
defined, 192
How Do You Leave and Where Do You
Go? exercise, 199–200
three forms of (past, future,
elsewhere), 195–200
Abyss, facing, 97–101
Action, taking, 106–31, 229
about: overview/takeaway of taking,
107, 131
bandwidth issue, 112–15
deciding to wait on next big thing,
115–16
exercises. *See* Action exercises
goal setting and, 126
at lunch time, 126
making time for, 117–23
marking milestones, 111–12
moving from thinking to doing,
117–23
overinvesting and, 128–30
schedule/time analysis for, 118–23
starting at the start, 107–9
starting calendar for, 117
value of, 116–17
What's In Your Way? quiz, 109–10
What's Your Bandwidth? quiz,
112–13
working smarter, not harder, 125–26
Action exercises
Book It, 115–16
Fill the Gaps, 127
Finding the Time, 118–23
Marking Milestones, 111–12
Overinvest in Your Vision, 129
Amanda, 18–19, 20, 73–74, 92–93, 137–
38, 139–41

Bandwidth issue, 112–15
Beginnings
challenges of, 107
starting at the start, 107–9
Book overview, 24–26, 226–34

Calendar, starting, 117. *See also* Time
Celebrating victories, 181–86
Cerberus. *See* Three-headed monster
Chuck, 44–45, 108–9, 116

Consequences
defined, 149
flexible, 157
good, characteristics of, 157–58
reasonable, 157
sufficient, 157
triggers and, 149–53

Dana, 196
Deadlines, perfectionism and, 164–66
Disempowerment, 163–64

Elsewhere, absence and, 198–99
E-mail efficiency, 125–26
Excellence, perfectionsim versus, 158,
162

Fear
choosing between Statement of
Purpose and, 103–4
facing the abyss, 97–101
statemement of, 101–3
Future, absence and, 196–98

Goals, setting, 126

Hero. *See* Inner hero; Love
Honor, Now and, 200–202

Imagining yourself (play and
imagination), 47–67, 228
about: overview and takeaway, 48, 67
benefits/importance of, 22, 23,
50–51, 54
Do You Play? quiz, 51–52
exercises. *See* Imagining yourself
(play and imagination) exercises
freedom, boundaries and, 58–59
Mr. Rogers' Neighborhood and
imagination, 60
need for, 48, 51
play as way of connecting, 55–57
playing as adults, 57–58
play space, 61–62
play tools, 63–65
quizzes, 51–52, 53–54
what play is and is not, 49–50
What's In the Way of Play? quiz,
53–54
where and when you will imagine,

62–63
  words, etc. getting in the way, 65–66
  work versus play, 49
  work without play, 57
Imagining yourself (play and
  imagination) exercises
  What Are Your Play Tools?, 66
  When Will You Imagine?, 62
  Where Will You Imagine?, 62
"Imperfections", 178–81
Inner critic, 84–105, 229
  about: overview and takeaway, 85,
    105
  choosing between Statement of
    Purpose and Fear, 103–4
  defeating, 94–104
  exercises. See Inner critic exercises
  facing the abyss, 97–101
  how you see yourself on inside,
    86–88
  identifying, 88–89
  moving from thinking to doing,
    85–86
  seeds of, 89–90
  separating from, 92–93
  sizing up, 91
  Statemement of Fear and, 101–3
  turning up volume on, 95–98
  Who's in Charge, Thoughts or
    Feelings? quiz, 98–100
Inner critic exercises
  Break It Up—Break It Down, 97–98
  Choose, 104
  The Inside You, 86–87
  Size Him Up, 91
  Turn Up the Volume on Your Inner
    Critic, 96–97
  Your Statement of Fear, 101–2
Inner hero, 170–87, 231. See also Love
  about: overview and takeaway, 171,
    187
  celebrating victories, 181–86
  self-preservation and, 171–72

Jason, 215–16
Joy
  activities of, discovering, 40–43
  leading with, 44–45
  past activities of, 43
  Past Activities of Joy exercise, 43

What Are Your Activities of Joy?
  quiz, 41
who you are and, 31

Knowing yourself, 30–46, 228. See also
  Joy
  about: overview and takeaway, 31, 46
  exercises. See Knowing yourself
    exercises
  roles you play, 31, 32–35
  values you hold, 31, 35–40
Knowing yourself exercises
  Past Activities of Joy, 43
  Performing Your Roles, 34–35
  What Are Your Roles?, 33–34
  What Are Your Values?, 36–39

Lance, 197–98
Living in the Now, 188–206
LIVING IN THE NOW, 231
Living in the Now
  about: overview and takeaway,
    189–90, 206
  Back to the Present exercise, 204–5
  Do You Live in the Now? quiz, 190–91
  importance of, 194
  strategies for (honor, presence,
    meditation), 200–205
  ways of escaping the Now, 192
  Where Am I Now? exercise, 202–3
Love
  conditional, perfectionism and, 163
  "imperfections" and, 178–81
  lessons of, 175–81
  The Meaning of Love exercise,
    176–77
  self-love, 172–75, 177–81
  What's Self-Love Got to Do with It?
    quiz, 173–74

Meditation, Now and, 203–5
Milestones, marking, 111–12
Moving with purpose, 220–35
  about: overview and takeaway, 221,
    235
  Checking In quiz, 222–24
  knowing versus walking your path,
    221–22
  Reviewing the Ten Steps exercise,
    226–32

Mr. Rogers' Neighborhood, 60

Overinvesting, 128–30

Passivity, 146–53
    choosing triggers, 153
    conscious decision for, 146
    consequences and, 149, 157–58
    distraction temptations and, 146
    Passive or Active? quiz, 147–48
    procrastination and, 149
    triggers and, 149–53
    What Are Your Triggers exercise,
        150–52
Past, absence and, 195–96
Perfectionism, 158–66
    Are You a Perfectionist? quiz, 159–61
    conditional love and, 163
    deadines eliminating, 164–66
    disempowerment and, 163–64
    downside of, 158
    excellence versus, 158, 162
    roots of, 162–64
Peter, 156, 157–58, 201–2
Play. *See* Imagining yourself (play and
    imagination)
Presence, Now and, 202–3
Process, embracing, 132–44, 230
    about: overview and takeaway, 133,
        144
    A Bend in the Road or the End of the
        Road? quiz, 134–36
    Reframing exercise, 139–43
    results orientation versus process
        orientation, 138, 140, 142
Procrastination, 153–58
    consequences and, 149, 157–58
    passivity and, 149
    triggers and, 149–53
    What Kind of Procrastinator Are
        You? quiz, 154–55
Purpose, discovering, 68–81, 228.
    See also Moving with purpose;
    Statemement of Purpose
    about: overview and takeaway, 69, 81
    exercises. *See* Purpose, exercises to
        discover
    purpose guiding actions and, 69–70
    value of discovering, 23–24, 69
    your legacy and, 71–74

Purpose, exercises to discover
    No Limits, 70–71
    Nothing Left to Lose, 74–75
    Your Great-Great-Granddaughter,
        72–73
    Your Statement of Purpose, 77–80

Quizzes
    about: guidelines for taking, 13
    Are You Absent?, 192–95
    Are You a Perfectionist?, 159–61
    A Bend in the Road or the End of the
        Road?, 134–36
    Checking In, 222–24
    Do You Live in the Now?, 190–91
    Do You Play?, 51–52
    Passive or Active?, 147–48
    Running in Place as Lifestyle?,
        19–20
    Running in Place at Work?, 14–15
    Running in Place in Relationships?,
        16–17
    Running with Vision?, 21–22
    What Are Your Activities of Joy?,
        41–42
    What Kind of Procrastinator Are
        You?, 154–55
    What's In the Way of Play?, 53–54
    What's In Your Way?, 109–10
    What's Self-Love Got to Do with It?,
        173–74
    What's Your Bandwidth?, 112–13
    Where Are You Now?, 209–11
    Who's in Charge, Thoughts or
        Feelings?, 98–100

Reggie, 182–83, 184, 232–33
Results orientation versus process
    orientation, 136–38, 140, 142
Review, of ten steps, 226–32
Roles you play, 31, 32–35
Running in place (being stuck)
    about: overview and takeaway, 12, 27
    getting moving with purpose, 22–26.
        See also Action, taking
    as lifestyle, 18–20
    play and, 22, 23
    purpose and, 23–24
    quizzes, 14–15, 16–17, 19–20, 21–22
    in relationships, 16–17

Running in Place as Lifestyle? quiz, 19–20
Running in Place at Work? quiz, 14–15
Running in Place in Relationships? quiz, 16–17
Running with Vision? quiz, 21–22
with vision, 20–22
at work, 14–15
work and, 23, 24

Self-knowledge. See Knowing yourself
Self-love. See Love
Senses, connecting with Now and, 203–4
Sharing yourself, 207–19, 231
about: overview and takeaway, 208, 219
Beneficiaries and Needs exercise, 216–17
how to do it, 212–17
questions to answer before, 217–18
reasons for, 211–12
resources, beneficiaries and needs, 212–17
Where Are You Now? quiz, 209–11
Where Are Your Resources? exercise, 213
Statemement of Fear, 101–3
Statemement of Purpose
bandwidth issue and, 112–15
choosing between Statement of Fear and, 103–4
creating, 75–80
Steps to take, 24–26, 226–32. See also specific steps
Stress
consequences and, 157
as good thing, 127
right amount of, 127

Tara, 55–56, 225–26
Technology sabbath, 125
Theresa, 64–65, 124
Three-headed monster, 146–67, 230. See also Passivity; Perfectionism; Procrastination; Triggers
about: overview and takeaway, 146, 167
consequences and, 149, 157–58
Passive or Active? quiz, 147–48

Time
calendar for managing, 117
deadlines, perfectionism and, 164–66
on duty versus off duty, 125
e-mail efficiency and, 125–26
Fill the Gaps exercise, 127
Finding the Time exercise, 118–23
lunch hour efficiency, 126
making, for action, 117–23
swap, 126
working smarter, not harder, 125–26
Triggers
choosing, 153
consequences and, 149, 157–58
defined, 149
using, to push past obstacles, 153, 155–57
What Are Your Triggers exercise, 150–52

Values you hold, 31, 35–40
Victories, celebrating, 181–86
Vision. See also Imagining yourself
importance of, 20
overinvesting in, 128–30
Running with Vision? quiz, 21–22
setting goals and, 126
ten steps to widen, 25–26
work and, 23, 24. See also Work

Work
defined, 23
on duty versus off duty, 125
efficiency at, leaving time for what's next, 124
e-mail efficiency, 125–26
function of, 24
lunch hour efficiency, 126
setting goals and, 126
smarter, not harder, 125–26
stress and, 127, 157
technology sabbath, 125
time swap, 126
without play, 57

ABOUT THE AUTHOR »

Dr. Ben Michaelis graduated *summa cum laude* from Columbia University (Columbia College) in 1995. He earned his Master's degree from New York University in 2001 and received his PhD in 2004, also from NYU. He has been the recipient of numerous academic distinctions, including a MacCracken Graduate Fellowship. Dr. Michaelis completed his clinical internship at New York University–Bellevue Hospital in 2004.

Dr. Michaelis has been in private practice in New York City since 2005. Since that time he has authored numerous scholarly articles and served on the faculty of Lenox Hill Hospital. He is currently a Visiting Scholar at Columbia University. His writing has been featured on the *Huffington Post* and Psychology Today.com, as well as many other websites and magazines. Dr. Michaelis has been a guest on various radio and nationally syndicated television programs. He lives with his family in Brooklyn, New York.